YOU
ON TOP

YOU
ON TOP

Smart, Sexy Skills
Every Woman Needs to
Set the World on Fire

KATE WHITE

WARNER BOOKS

NEW YORK   BOSTON

Warner Books
Hachette Book Group USA
237 Park Avenue
New York, NY 10169
Visit our Web site at www.HachetteBookGroupUSA.com

Printed in the United States of America

Originally published in hardcover by Warner Books as *How to Set His Thighs on Fire*

First Trade Edition: June 2007
10 9 8 7 6 5 4 3 2 1

LCCN: 2006036949
ISBN: 978-0-446-69552-7

TABLE OF CONTENTS

INTRODUCTION

It was the weirdest phenomenon and I couldn't figure out what was causing it. Several years ago I started to receive e-mails—and letters, too—from guys I'd once dated but hadn't set eyes on in years. The message was pretty much the same with each one: *Hi, how are you, I just wanted to write and see how you were doing after all this time.* They'd mention what they were up to professionally, how many rug rats they were raising, and a few other tidbits. Some of them were guys I'd had only a few dates with; others had been more serious crushes. There was even one letter—a Christmas card, actually, with a schmaltzy illustration of a horse-drawn sleigh charging through the snow— from this real bad boy who'd stomped on my heart so hard you wouldn't think he even *believed* in Christmas. I'd never expected to hear from him again in this lifetime.

Why are they doing this? I wondered. Maybe, I thought jokingly, there's some kind of nostalgia hormone that floods the male body after the age of forty. Another possibility was that their daughters were all going to want internships in the magazine business at some point and the fathers were laying the foundation.

Then, one day, somebody offered me an explanation I'd never considered. I was catching up over lunch with a male editor who used to work for me, and I mentioned the phenomenon just to get his take on it. No sooner was the story out of my mouth than he tossed his head back and laughed out loud.

"Kate, are you nuts?" he said, when he was done chortling. "Don't you see the real reason they're getting in touch?"

"Obviously not," I replied.

"I'll tell you exactly why they're doing it," he said. "They think you know all this amazing stuff about sex now because you're the editor in chief of *Cosmo*. They're totally intrigued."

I burst into laughter. I wasn't at all sure whether he was right but it amused me greatly to think of some former minor boyfriend perusing *Cosmo* coverlines like "How to Touch a Naked Man" and "Sex He'll Go Wild For: Awesome New Bed Tricks That Actually Double His Pleasure," thinking he'd give me a call in the hope I might share what I'd learned.

Well, I won't be sharing that wisdom with any of them. But I have to admit that I *have* learned a ton in the years I've been editing *Cosmo*. Yes, some tantalizing facts about sex because that's one of our specialties. But I've also learned a lot about men, love, human behavior, success, office politics, and just plain life in general. Some of it I've gleaned as I've been editing all the articles we've run on those subjects; other tidbits I've picked up from the fascinating people I've met and the intriguing situations I've found myself in. I feel like a big sponge absorbing this amazing stuff that I would never have learned otherwise. My job at *Cosmopolitan*—whether I'm dropping into a cover shoot, giving a luncheon for an author, or writing *Cosmo* coverlines—would be incredibly exhilarating regardless, but picking up all this information has been a terrific bonus.

When Your Boss Calls, Jump

The funny thing is I never even applied to be the editor in chief of *Cosmo*, and when the job was first offered to me, I was nearly knocked over by a wave of ambivalence. It all began on a Sunday in August, while I was relaxing at a weekend home my husband and I have in Pennsylvania (to be honest, I was baking a blueberry pie for my family, which in hindsight seems like a really absurd thing to be doing the day you're tapped to run a magazine like *Cosmo*). The phone rang; I picked it up with floury hands and was shocked to hear the voice of my boss, the president of our magazine division. She sounded peppy on the phone, so I was pretty sure I wasn't about to be canned; yet, on the other hand, it was highly unusual for her to phone me on a Sunday, so I knew something major was cooking (besides my damn pie).

"What's up?" I inquired, my legs going all rubbery on me.

She asked me to drive into the city and meet with her that very afternoon. She had something special to share with me, something she thought I'd like. I was running *Redbook* magazine at the time and the first thought that flashed through my mind was, *Oh shit, I'm not the editor of* Redbook *anymore.*

Leaving my husband and kids behind, I headed back to Manhattan. In the car I ran through possible scenarios in my head and even rehearsed dialogue in the hopes that I wouldn't say anything dim-witted when informed of my new professional lot in life.

"Kate, we'd like you to run our New Media office," I dejectedly imagined my boss announcing to me.

"Great, great," I would reply, while fighting the urge to dry-heave. "It sounds like a wonderful opportunity."

As soon as I arrived in my boss's office, she asked me to sit down. It was clear that whatever was going to happen would happen mercifully fast. Within four seconds of my fanny hitting the seat cushion, she told me that the company was offering me the job as editor in chief of *Cosmopolitan* magazine. I was absolutely dumbfounded—she might as well have announced that the company wanted me to fly a hot-air balloon over the Atlantic as part of a corporate promotion. The current *Cosmo* editor, who had taken over when Helen Gurley Brown retired, had been in the job only a year and a half, and I hadn't heard even a morsel of gossip suggesting she would be jumping ship. As soon as I recovered from my initial shock, two feelings rushed through me like water through a hose. One was pure exhilaration. I was being handed the chance to run the most successful women's magazine in the world—and I hadn't even had to go through the typical torturous recruitment process in which you prepare a million ideas for the magazine and wait weeks for the company to get back to you. It would be thrilling to head *Cosmo*. The challenge would be an instant antidote to the mild career malaise I'd been experiencing over the past year or so.

But at the same moment I also felt pure terror. I'd been the editor in chief of several national magazines and had a good track record, so I was certain that I'd be able to handle the day-to-day responsibilities that came with overseeing a big magazine. But I worried that *Cosmo* wasn't the right match for me. In my most recent jobs I'd been editing for a reader who was older, married rather than single, and not nearly as feisty as the *Cosmo* girl. I wondered if I'd be able to make the magazine as exciting as it had to be. Plus, there was so much at stake. I knew from being in the company that American *Cosmo* was important not only because it sold tons on the newsstand every month, but also because there were many successful international editions, all relying on material from the U.S. version. If I bombed, it would be like a horrible game of dominoes—my failure might soon spread to *Cosmo* in Australia, China, Thailand, Russia, Turkey, Poland, France, Argentina—everywhere. Messing up might very well be against the laws of the Geneva Convention!

My only option, however, was to tell my boss yes. In the seven seconds I bought in which to make a decision—by saying "Wow" four or five times and asking where my predecessor was going (lured away by another company, it turned out)—I knew that it would be insane to turn down the offer. My excitement outdistanced my anxiety, and I just kept telling myself over and over that I would have to figure out a way to pull it off.

Sex and the Single Girl

That night I tossed and turned till dawn, ricocheting between exuberance over the prize I'd been given and anxiety about handling the enormous challenge before me. At least when you *apply* for a job, you have the opportunity to cogitate about what you'd do in the position—and in my business, what direction you'd take the magazine in. I hadn't had the chance to do that. Yet despite my trepidation, I realized that perhaps my path had been heading toward *Cosmo* all along. I'd had a few intriguing foreshadowings.

The first one was when I was just sixteen and busy musing about my future. My mother gave me a copy of Helen Gurley Brown's classic bestseller, *Sex and the Single Girl*, which had been published several years before. She told me, "Ignore the advice in the book, but *be* like her." What she was saying, in other words, was, "Don't go out and have wild, single-girl sex, but since I know that you have a dream of working in magazines someday, Helen Gurley Brown is the perfect role model."

My mother was right in that I had long fantasized about one day scoring a job in magazine publishing, and her advice to me was both helpful and inspiring. But neither she nor I ever realized I'd one day take it so freaking *literally*.

My next *Cosmo* prophetic moment involved the legendary Helen herself. I managed to break into the magazine business after college by winning *Glamour* magazine's Top Ten College Women contest and appearing on the cover. After several low-level jobs in the industry, I became a senior editor at a weekly newspaper supplement similar to *Parade*, reporting to this fabulous editor named Art Cooper (who later went on to reinvent *GQ*). One day Art called me into his office and announced that he wanted me to interview Helen Gurley Brown for the Q&A page, where we frequently featured authors. "She's got this new book coming out," he told me. "And besides, I think it would be good for you to meet her. I could really see you in her job someday."

I was flattered by Art's comment. It would be great to have the opportunity to meet Helen, though I couldn't imagine filling her shoes one day. I just didn't seem much like a *Cosmo* girl.

I went to interview Helen in her chintz-and-leopard-print office, and here's the amazing thing. We were wearing *identical outfits*. I don't mean *sort of* alike. I mean identical. We each had on flowy black pants, a drapey, long-sleeved white blouse, and a little black ribbon tied in a bow around our necks. Okay, her blouse was probably silk Chanel and mine was made of the kind of cheap polyester that smells like kerosene when it's the slightest bit damp, but to the untrained eye we were twins! *How odd*, I remember thinking as I sat across from her. (She didn't seem to notice.)

A few years later when I was an articles editor at another magazine, Helen actually called me up and asked me to come over and talk to her. I'm not sure how I ended up in her line of sight, but she said she wanted to discuss my coming to work for her. The magazine, she said, needed fresh blood at the top. I had just been promoted and didn't want a *new* job (are you beginning to suspect a pattern on my part of protesting too much?), but I liked having the chance to talk to her again. In the end she said she didn't want to hire me but the reason floored me.

"It wouldn't be a good idea, Kate," she said. "I think you could *run* this magazine someday. And so if I hired you, you'd get here and in a few years you'd be dying to take over my job. But I don't plan to retire for at least ten years [it was almost fifteen years later before she did], and so you'd be terribly restless and bored."

Maybe all those funny little *Cosmo* moments had been trying to tell me something.

Karma Sutra and Beyond

I fell out of bed the next morning, finished up business at *Redbook*, and just a few days later was fully ensconced at *Cosmo*. The first months on the job were absolutely nutty. Several dozen people resigned during this time, most of them to join the former editor in chief at her new job but others bailed because they didn't want to go through another round of changes. I was afraid that at any moment I'd find myself putting out the magazine with only seven other people, just like the way I used to put on talent shows in my backyard.

Also, because *Cosmo* has more editorial pages than most other magazines, the volume of work was much greater than what I was used to. There were plenty of moments when I was racing around like the proverbial chicken with its head cut off.

There's one story that sums up perfectly how frenzied I felt during the first months. One day, to my complete horror, I suspected that I might be pregnant (not something I had planned). I bought a home pregnancy test and took it in the private bathroom that Helen Brown had installed. According to the instructions on the box, the results would appear in just sixty seconds. And you know what I thought? *Great, sixty seconds—I'll use that time to do something else.* I left the bathroom and raced over to the art department to sign off on some layouts. And I became so immersed in what I was doing that I forgot to go back and check the results. I didn't realize until I arrived home later that I never looked at the stick. (I had to wait until the next day to, with relief, discover the minus sign.)

But eventually the staff stabilized, I filled the vacant positions with my own team, and I adjusted to the volume of work. And it was then that I began to discover how much I loved my job. Because *Cosmo* is a magazine that's edgy and a little over the top, it was easy to attract dynamic people to work there, and being around them every day was an absolute blast. Also, running a magazine with such iconic status offered me amazing access and opportunities. Perfect example: a few months after I started, Donald Trump called to invite me to lunch so he could tell me about a modeling agency he was involved in. After a fantastic meal at the four-star Jean Georges restaurant, where the staff did everything short of massage my calves, Donald suggested that we skip dessert so he could show me something interesting. We jumped into his stretch limo, drove across town, and he took me up to the top floor of one of the buildings he was in the midst of constructing. He said he thought I'd get a kick out of seeing the view and meeting some of the construction guys he worked with. It kind of makes me a precursor to one of the candidates on *The Apprentice*, doesn't it?

All sorts of opportunities like this fell in my lap because of the job, though sometimes I made *sure* they happened—like when we were shooting Hugh Grant for a story. I told the art director I would drop by the studio that day because Hugh was an extremely important celebrity and I wanted to be sure everything was going perfectly. Yeah, right. By the way, he's just as hunky in person as he is on screen.

Best of all, though, was discovering how much I loved working on the actual content of the magazine. It was fun, gutsy, and inspiring. When Helen Gurley Brown revitalized *Cosmopolitan* in 1965, from a dull about-to-fold general interest magazine (she'd been given the chance because of the success of her book), she had a very clear mission in mind: to make it the single girl's bible. Through the second half of the century, *Cosmo* reassured women that they could have a hunky guy, a hot career, and plenty of happiness if they were willing to work for it. It ran articles that tried to boost their confidence and teach them what they needed to know.

I was smart enough to realize that the basic formula still made sense, and I didn't tinker with it. We're still about living large and being on top of your game—whether in love, sex, or life. We give readers plenty of strategies for doing so—strategies for work, style, personal growth, and perhaps most important, for men and relationships. As one of my editors says, at *Cosmo*, we're fluent in dude.

It's been nearly nine years and I still find each moment at *Cosmo* thrilling. There's not a single day when I don't learn at least ten new things.

So here are eighty-six of my favorite strategies for being on top—from how to make a dazzling impression, to how to get a man to open up, to how to keep sex with your partner extremely hot.

I hope these lessons prove as useful for you as they have for me.

YOU
ON TOP

PART ONE

YOU ON TOP

Starting Now

ONE

How to Figure Out What You Want in Life

I guess you could say I was lucky because from the time I was young I had a fairly clear idea that I wanted to be a writer and editor one day, and that meant I didn't have to lurch around in my twenties figuring out my destiny. I composed lots of silly plays, poetry, and short stories as a kid, and though at first I wasn't sure what type of writer I wanted to be, eventually I started reading magazines and began fantasizing about one day living in a cute little apartment in Manhattan and working for a women's magazine.

Nowadays they call it having a vision for your future, but back then it was simply thought of as knowing what you wanted to do when you grew up. Some people just have a sense from an early age what their destiny is. When I met Cyndi Lauper at a recent luncheon, I asked her when she realized that she had a unique voice and would become a singer. "At two," she said. Celebrity stylist Rachel Zoe, who writes a fashion column for us, says that as early as second grade, it was pretty clear she was going to be a stylist. She went through the closet of a boy she was friends with and laid out a week's worth of clothes for him to wear to school because she didn't think he dressed hip enough.

I never felt smug because I had my career epiphany so early, but I was grateful. When I reached my twenties, I met more than a few people who still weren't sure what they wanted to do with their lives and were frustrated because of it.

But eventually I came to see that it doesn't matter a whole lot if you're one of the early birds. People who figure out their calling later can be just as happy and successful. And besides, an early epiphany takes you only so far in life. Over time you change and your desires may change, too. Even if, at age twenty-four, you are absolutely positive of what you want, you may find yourself restless and yearning for something new at thirty-five—and not at all sure what that should be.

I've experienced that a couple of times during my professional life, before I got to *Cosmo*. At one point my restlessness was so pronounced that I consulted with a career coach for guidance. She suggested I go home, take out a piece of paper, and write down the answer to the following question: "What's missing?" It was an interesting assignment, but I didn't make much progress with it. I knew I was missing a sense of accomplishment and excitement in my work, and yet I didn't know how to generate them.

I followed up with a few other strategies. For instance, I dug out a legal pad and made a list of my likes and dislikes. I took a daylong seminar in which I and the other participants were encouraged to nearly talk ourselves to death in order to discover what really lit our fire. I thumbed through a few books on the subject, too, including *What Color Is Your Parachute?* which has sold about six billion copies. It offers a workbook in the back that is supposed to guide you to your true calling, but the thought of filling it out seemed as appealing as washing a mountain of panty hose by hand.

Fast-forward a couple of years. I was still in magazines (not at

Cosmo yet), but also writing a book about successful women, listening each day to different ones describe their passion and how they managed to turn it into a brilliant career. Since I had reached a decent level of success in my own life, I wasn't expecting to learn anything staggeringly new from these women. But when I was all done with my research, I realized there was a fascinating common denominator among most of the women. They had discovered what lit their fire not by thinking, journaling, filling out worksheets, or talking ad nauseam, but by *bumping into it* somewhere—while seeing a play, for instance, or traveling, or admiring a necklace someone was wearing, or visiting a friend's workplace, or in one case while riding the L in Chicago.

But it wasn't until I arrived at *Cosmo* that this fact really crystallized for me—partly because of a charming story my original fashion director, Elaine D'Farley, told me. I asked Elaine why she had pursued a career in fashion, expecting her to say that she'd always loved that world and had studied at the Fashion Institute of Technology, like lots of girls in her field. But she said she'd actually been an art major in college and after graduation had been clueless about her calling in life. For lack of anything better to do, she had followed a boyfriend to Egypt, and one day while out exploring, they came upon a team from a European magazine shooting a fashion story. She was mesmerized as she watched the fashion stylist work, and even ended up holding one of the light reflectors.

"I knew right then that I wanted to be a fashion stylist," she told me. "I guess you have to be on a bus to Cairo to figure out what you want."

The way she said it was so damn poetic but also summed up what I'd learned from all those women: the best way to figure out what you're yearning for is not to talk yourself hoarse or think so hard you blow a gasket in your brain but to board a bus—literally as well as figuratively. The point is to just try lots of new and different things so that you have plenty of opportunity to meet up with your passion. Fly the ocean in a silver plane, visit galleries, take classes (though not necessarily in what you *think* you're looking for but something offbeat instead), make lunch dates with intriguing people you've met but never thought you'd call. Trust me, if you keep doing this, at some unexpected moment, something will call out to you.

TWO

Toss Out Your Five-Year Plan

Has anyone ever asked you, "Where do you see yourself five years from now?" It's a question that used to be routinely tossed out by prospective bosses during job interviews. You were supposed to offer an answer that disclosed intense ambition on your part—though you had to be careful not to drool with greed as you talked, or look voraciously at the desk of the person conducting the interview!

People don't ask that question as often as they used to, but it still pops up—not only in job interviews but also when friends are brainstorming with you about your future. Do you see yourself married in five years? Having kids? Running a company? You're supposed to give an answer.

I've come to believe, though, that plotting out your life in five- or ten- or twenty-year installments isn't necessarily very helpful, and even has the potential to thwart you. I'm not suggesting you just wing it or stumble along purposelessly. It's important to have a rough sense of the things you want in life and how you'd like to unfurl your fabulous talents. When you mentally declare things like "I want children someday" or "I won't be truly happy unless I have my picture taken in front of the Taj Mahal," it sets a course for you and encourages you to make choices that over time facilitate those desires. But there's a danger in being so locked into a life scheme that you miss an opportunity that's smack-dab in the

7

road in front of you or a new adventure that beckons you from a mysterious side road off to the right or left. A line of philosopher Joseph Campbell's sums it up so beautifully: "We must be willing to get rid of the life we've planned, so as to have the life that is waiting for us."

I really started to think hard about this issue after I'd fallen in love with my current job. If there was one thing I knew for sure when I'd been offered the position, it was that I'd never fantasized about being the editor of *Cosmo* and in fact, couldn't quite picture myself in the job even as it was being presented to me. But the dubious part of my brain was overridden by a part that was intrigued, hungry for change, curious about a new adventure, and I confess, exhilarated at the thought of being able to tell people what I did for a living. Being so happy in a job I once couldn't have imagined accepting has been proof to me that there's a risk in holding too firmly to a long-term plan.

A rigid five- or ten- or twenty-year plan can not only prevent you from being receptive to unexpected opportunities, but it can also depress the hell out of you if it doesn't pan out. I have a friend who has her heart set on a certain job, the end-point position that you can reach in her field. More and more, though, it's looking as if it's not in the cards for her—maybe she's not political enough or not cut out for it after all or maybe she just didn't end up in the right place at the right time. She's very talented and hardworking and could probably flourish in a slightly different field, but she's unwilling to give up that old dream she had for herself. And it's really bumming her out.

Since I've come to *Cosmo*, what I've decided works best for me is to live a *little* ahead of myself—kind of like the way your cell phone roams for service when you are outside of your designated territory. I try to keep my ears perked and mind open.

I've torn up my five- and ten-year plans and instead I keep a crazy list on my BlackBerry of all the fascinating things that I *might* want to try one day—like living in Provence with my husband or studying forensics at John Jay College of Criminal Justice. Consider keeping a list like that instead of a definitive plan. Over time you can explore the items that intrigue you the most and then decide if they still grab you or not.

Also, never say no to any opportunity until you've considered it for at least twenty-four hours. If you're in a muddle, ask yourself, *Despite the fact that this is making me feel anxious or uncomfortable, is there a chance my life might become more interesting and exciting if I said yes?*

THREE

Don't Believe Everything You Think

After I got the *Cosmo* job, there was one thing that haunted me for months: the job had turned out to be such a perfect fit for me, and yet I knew, beyond a shadow of a doubt, that if the position hadn't been offered cold to me and the company had instead announced a major search for an editor in chief, I would never have thrown my hat into the ring. I wouldn't have thought that the job would appeal to me or that I'd be considered the right candidate.

Why did that knowledge haunt me? Because I'd always thought that I was capable of making a fair assessment of my strengths and weaknesses as well as my true needs and desires. It perturbed me that other people (all the executives in the company who'd weighed in) had so clearly seen an ideal opportunity for me whereas I would have been blind to it. I wanted to figure out how to prevent myself from being so obtuse in the future.

I finally came to accept, however, that we don't always view ourselves accurately and we don't necessarily know what's best for us. When we're at a crossroads in life or trying to evaluate what step to take, we shouldn't necessarily believe what we think. In certain instances we may be dead wrong. Other people may actually know better than we do.

So how can you tell when what you believe *is* right and when it's dangerously off the mark?

After torturing myself for months, here's what I've decided. First, it helps to listen to little things people say about you. Not mean-spirited, catty comments, but remarks (off the cuff ones, too) from pals, bosses, and even casual acquaintances that run against the grain of what you've been telling yourself. We did an interview with Matthew McConaughey in 2005, and I was struck by this one little story he told. After he'd broken into films and was finally earning decent money, he hired a maid to come to his place every other day. One night he described to a friend how great it was to have maid service and the fact that the woman even ironed his jeans. His friend replied, "That's cool—if you *want* your jeans ironed." McConaughey said that he thought about it and realized that no, actually, he *didn't* really want or need his jeans ironed. And it made him think about all the other things he didn't really need in life. He said that since then he's tended to live pretty simply.

While I was brooding about my lack of self-awareness I remembered a telling incident. When Helen Gurley Brown retired from *Cosmo*, the job of editor in chief went to someone else, who held it for eighteen months. After Helen's replacement was announced, a man in my company pulled me aside and asked if I was upset. "Gosh, no," I said without a morsel of insincerity. But in hindsight, I should have noodled over his comment. *Could* I have been a candidate? What did he see in me that I was oblivious to?

It also helps to pump friends for feedback and advice. Let's say you feel at a crossroads in your life and aren't sure what to do. Ask a friend, "Where do *you* see me next?" or "What do *you* think would make me happy at this point in my life?" The answer may reveal an appreciation of a strength of yours that you haven't acknowledged or have always pooh-poohed. Or they may bring up a dream you mentioned years ago but put aside.

Of course, you have to ask the right friend, someone who has always had your back and doesn't feel any instinct to undermine you. At my first magazine job there was a woman one level up whom I considered my role model. She was a respected writer, not brilliant but clever and super industrious. I was thrilled when my writing started to earn raves just as hers did. One day she pulled me aside and told me she had figured out exactly what I should do with my life. I nearly panted in anticipation, hoping that she was about to say something like "I see you becoming a star writer and turning out bestselling books that get made into movies with Robert Redford in the male lead." Instead she announced, "I think you should run for Congress one day." It nearly knocked the wind out of me.

Another strategy is to dare to challenge your own thinking and turn it on its ear. Ask yourself, *Why* do I believe that? *Why* do I think that will make me happy? *Why* don't I think I could handle that? Martha Beck, a wonderful life coach and author of *Finding Your Own North Star: Claiming the Life You Were Meant to Live*, told me that in order to figure out where our real desires lie, we need to separate our essential self from the socialized self. "The essential self responds to what's innate and intuitive," she says. Or in other words, what we really love doing. The socialized self, on the other hand, gets caught up in compliance with what *other* people want from us. "We have a fear of social consequences so we modify our behavior to please others."

Hindsight can be a good tool for tapping into the essential self. Think about what made you feel good in the past, what left you with a feeling of bliss. That's what you should be aiming for. Consider what your life would be like if you do more of *that* thing. Play this game, Beck suggests: ask yourself, When time flies, what is it that I'm doing? Then imagine someone calling you up and offering you the opportunity to do that as much as you desire. Now look for a job or situation that comes as close to that as possible as opposed to the one you may *think* you need.

FOUR

Almost *Anything* Can Benefit from Some Added Sex Appeal

As I've said before, during the past few years I've thought a lot about sexiness. Mostly it's been in relation to helping women know what nabs a guy's attention—what kind of hair is sexy, for instance, or what kind of words, when whispered in his ear, will work him into a frenzy. But as I've given so much thought to the subject, I've come to realize that sex appeal matters in far more situations than just guy-girl dynamics, and that there are tons of instances in which it pays to make something *sexier*. If, let's say, the PowerPoint presentations you give at work seem to lower the pulse of most of your audience, or you rarely hear back when you send out a résumé, or the people you meet at parties are often eyeing the bar within forty-five seconds of the introduction, it's probably time to "sexify."

By "sexify" I don't mean making presentations dressed in a thong bikini or starting cover letters with phrases like "I hear you're a really hot boss and I'd love to show you my stuff." The word *sexy* today has a broader definition than being sexually suggestive or stimulating. *Sexy* means exciting, appealing, fascinating, captivating, intriguing, alluring, and ultimately *tempting*. When I work on coverlines, I try to make them as sexy as possible, and the question I always ask myself is: Are they intriguing enough to tempt a girl to walk across a crowded store and buy the issue? You could use the same criteria for many other things in life. Is your resumé intriguing enough to tempt a prospective employer to call you? Is your cocktail chatter so fascinating that it will tempt someone to stay even longer to talk to you? Will the cookies you donate to the school bake sale tempt someone to buy them? Is your invitation going to tempt people to come to your party or event? Will your opening statement at a meeting tempt everyone to listen closely?

You're probably thinking, *Well, of course I'm always aiming for that kind of response.* But we often pull back slightly in our efforts—out of self-consciousness or fear of seeming too forward or flashy. Adding just a little sex appeal can make all the difference.

Speaking of bake sales, not long after I landed the *Cosmo* job, my son needed me to make cupcakes for a bake sale fund-raiser at his school. I knew that plenty of the nonworking moms would be whipping up fabulous confections, but since I couldn't start my baking until after dinner and homework, I wouldn't be able to produce anything very magical. That was a bummer, because I wanted my son to be proud of his cupcakes, and for his sake, I wanted them to *sell*. I dashed out to buy chocolate cake mix and a few tubs of chocolate frosting, and as an afterthought, I picked up a huge container of colored sprinkles. Once the cupcakes had cooled, I laid the frosting on extra thick and piled on tons of sprinkles.

The next day I dropped off my son, along with the cupcakes, at the cafeteria where the bake sale was happening, and then delivered my daughter to her classroom. When I returned to the cafeteria a while later to see how things were going, I noticed a few kids stuffing my chocolate cupcakes into their mouths—and there were only *two* left on the platter. The cupcakes had sold like the proverbial hotcakes. Maybe they were made from a box mix, but I suddenly realized that with their mounds of chocolate icing and billions of carnival-colored sprinkles, they were the sexiest damn baked goods in the entire cafeteria.

Here are a few thoughts on sexifying:

- **Go for big—in size and numbers.** That's part of what makes *Cosmo* covers so sexy: big hair, big lips, big cleavage, big attitude—and big numbers, too, such as "101 Sex Tips" and "50 Fun Ways to Get Close to Him." Your living room might be sexier and more inviting with a whole bunch of chenille-covered throw pillows on the couch. Your résumé might be more compelling with a bigger typeface. Recently, I read a written critique of a magazine by a woman up for a major job in the industry. The font size she chose was much larger than normal and numerous sentences were in bold. I couldn't stop reading it.
- **Think red.** According to Lisa Herbert, executive VP of Pantone, a company that specializes in color communication technology, red sends a message that you are sexy and exciting.
- **Connect with your "audience" as much as possible.** When I write coverlines, I try to use the word *you* at least several times on a single cover. That's because people find it totally seductive when you're focusing on them. When you give a talk or a speech, mention what you believe to be concerns felt by your audience. Ask them questions.
- **Connect on a physical plane, too.** Offer a really firm hand-

shake and don't quickly yank your hand away. Hold eye contact, too.

I once had the opportunity to sit next to Bill Clinton at dinner—he liked my mysteries and had requested to meet me. Okay, the guy is so charismatic you feel some kind of force field when you're around him. People talk about his amazing eye contact and it's really true. He looks you in the eye and holds it, and it's a uniquely disconcerting but amazing experience. In fact, Bob Woodward, whom I met once at a luncheon, told me that when he interviewed Clinton during his presidency, Clinton did the eye-holding thing even while he downed a Diet Coke, and he kept his eyes on Woodward right through the bottom of the glass! You don't want to go overboard with it, but locking eyes with someone can have a powerful impact.

- **Tease.** Teasing has lots of sex appeal. And you don't have to do it just when you're dying to jump into bed with someone. A comment like "I have an idea that could save the company a ton of money—can we meet later to discuss it?" will work your boss into a lather.

FIVE

The Amount of Serendipity You Experience Is in Direct Proportion to the Amount of Time Your Butt Is off the Sofa

The most serendipitous thing that ever happened to me was one day, without any warning, being asked to take over the job as editor in chief of *Cosmo*. As I mentioned in the Introduction, I was just minding my own business on a Sunday afternoon, making a blueberry pie, when my boss called and asked if I'd drive into Manhattan from our weekend home so she could talk to me about an exciting development. Hours later, after I accepted the job offer and was headed home in a taxi, the question that kept flashing through my head was, *How in the world did I manage to score this incredible prize?*

Serendipity is the phenomenon of finding valuable or agreeable things not *sought* for. I hadn't applied for the *Cosmo* job. I'd never even hinted to anyone in the company that I'd be interested in it.

Yet, of course, it was no accident that I'd landed in a very big and delicious pot of jam. Weeks, months, even years before I received the offer, I had set certain wheels in motion. Over time I had performed in a way that made my bosses think I was right for the job. I *had* been a seeker, just not for the *Cosmo* job specifically.

As I lay in bed that Sunday night after my work life changed so dramatically, I wondered whether I'd done anything in particular that might have tipped the situation in my favor. A memory broke loose in my mind. A little over a year before, I'd been part of a team in our company that had been asked to generate an idea for a new magazine and present it at our management conference—mainly for the purpose of starting an interesting dialogue. At our first meeting I volunteered to be the team leader because no one else seemed eager for the chore. I wasn't thrilled to have the extra work but I felt it would be good for me to churn things up a bit in my professional life. I'd been feeling restless, borderline discontent. And when no one else jumped at the chance to make the actual presentation, I volunteered to do that, too.

It wasn't the world's most scintillating presentation but I must have made good points because afterwards my boss gave me a big smile and a thumbs-up. I sensed that she not only liked my effort but also saw me in a new way that day. Was *that* the moment, I wondered, when she'd first envisioned a bigger future for me?

I don't know the answer. But I do know that when I view all the serendipitous things that have happened to me, I see that they're all a result of hauling my butt off the sofa at a given moment.

Every time you talk to a new person at a party, hear a lecture on a subject you're unfamiliar with, invite a new acquaintance to have a drink with you, or take on an extra project or challenge at work, you boost the chance of serendipity in your life.

SIX

Own Your Hotness

One of the things I've thought a lot about since I've been in my job is the whole notion of sexiness. We write frequently about being sexy and feeling sexy and just plain reveling in your own sexiness. We also always aim to make the magazine sexy *visually*. When I review photography with the art department, we frequently make comments like "That's really sexy" or "That's not sexy enough" or "This picture's sexier than the other one—let's go with that."

And, of course, our covers have to be the embodiment of sexiness. It's our signature, what's contributed to the iconic status of *Cosmo* covers for forty years. The bottom line: the more a cover radiates sex appeal, the better that issue sells.

I wish I could perfectly define what sexiness is, because then I'd be better able to hit the mark with covers each time—and not have the occasional newsstand dud. But, unfortunately, it's not so easy. For starters, what's sexy to one person isn't necessarily sexy to the next. And though there are some attributes usually linked with female sexiness—like full lips, long lustrous hair, and a curvy body—you can certainly be hot without any of them. Recently we were working on a story about Hollywood marriages—about both the winners and the losers in that game (one common denominator of those that work: the couples rarely spend more than two weeks apart). When we called in photos of some classic Hollywood couples, there was a shot among them of Frank Sinatra and Mia Farrow on their wedding day. She'd recently chopped off all her blonde hair into a kind of Twiggy cut and she was slender and gamine-like, so strikingly different from the other women Sinatra had dated. And not at all the classic definition of sexiness. In fact, at the time of the marriage, Ava Gardner, his former girlfriend, had reportedly declared, "I always knew he'd end up in bed with a boy."

And yet when I looked at that shot of Mia Farrow, all I could think was that she was totally sexy and enchanting. Frank Sinatra had certainly thought so. Farrow didn't have any of the classic attributes of sexiness. So what made her so compelling? I think she was sexy because she *believed* she was.

What I've really come to see in my job is that sexiness is first and foremost an attitude. It's *confidence*, a belief in your own allure. I see it again and again with both models and actresses. During the seventies and eighties, the *Cosmo* cover girl always had a come-hither expression on her face, as if she were looking at a guy and was about to utter something like "Get over here so I can tear your pants off with my teeth." But today I feel when we get the right cover image, it's as if the girl—model or actress—has just walked through the door into a party, scanned the crowd, and is thinking, *I so own this room.*

Here's a fascinating behind-the-scenes story that sums up just how much confidence is related to sex appeal. Though we shoot mostly actresses for our covers, occasionally we use models, and we generally go with someone who isn't what you'd call a supermodel yet. That's because we love to feature girls who aren't totally familiar to the reader, girls who come across as young and fresh and ready to take on the world. The trouble is when you are shooting a model who is young and fresh, chances are she hasn't done many covers yet, and she's likely to be pretty nervous at the shoot. She feels the pressure to not only look great, but also be divinely sexy—it's *Cosmo*, after all. With very few exceptions, the new models have a tough time beating down their anxiety, and that anxiety shows up on film. They look stiff and awkward, sometimes downright terrified. After I'd been at *Cosmo* a few months, I told my design director, Ann Kwong, that we had to figure out a way to make the cover shoots with models work better.

So we came up with interesting strategy. When we book a girl for a cover try, we have the modeling agency explain to her that someone rarely scores a cover the first time out and that the shoot should be thought of as mainly a warm-up exercise. That's sometimes enough to do the trick but not always. The film will come in and we might discover that the model has real potential but she was too much of a nervous Nellie. So here's what we do next. We call the modeling agency and tell them we want to reshoot the girl. But we never say that we need to do it again because the model looked so wigged out that the photos could be used as posters for *Scream 4*. What we say is that we love the girl but we aren't wild about the *clothes* we chose for her on the first shoot. The girl arrives at the next shoot completely at ease. And why not? She's under the impression that she looked totally sexy the first time—the only problem was the hideous red halter top or whatever she was wearing. And that changes everything. This time the girl exudes confidence and sex appeal. And the pictures are generally fabulous.

This process always reinforces for me just how much of sexiness is *mental*. The model looks amazingly sexy in the second batch of photos in large part because she *believes* she is—now that we've booked her again.

There are two morals to this story. The first is that even if you aren't cover-model hot, you can exude sexiness simply by believing you've got it.

Secondly, the best way to believe in your sexiness is to convince yourself of it rather than wait around for someone else to convince you. Too many women experience their hotness on kind of a rental basis—for instance when their husband or boyfriend pays them a compliment or guys turn their heads as they walk into a bar or the *Cosmo* design director books them for a second shoot. They don't *own* their hotness.

Remember Omarosa from *The Apprentice*? She was considered the evil one, of course, the conniving bitch, but I met her when I did a segment on the first *Apprentice* and I found her intriguing. After the show was over, I invited her to my house for dinner. One of the things that struck me about her was that she really believed in her own sexiness. She wasn't waiting around for someone to tell her. And because of this, she could light up a room. My dog, a little Westie, leapt into her arms when she arrived and then sat in her lap for the rest of the night. I have never, ever seen him act like that with anyone else. As far as he was concerned, she was on fire.

So *own* your hotness rather than rent it. Instead of waiting around for anyone to anoint you, anoint yourself. I know that it's far easier said than done, but you can start by vowing to not bash any single part of your looks. If the words "I hate my . . ." take a single step across your brain, just stop them. You also need to consider what your best asset is and play it up to the max: if it's your legs, wear short skirts and great shoes; if it's your long, lustrous hair, pay to have it blown out every week. And most important, decide on a moxie mantra you can say to yourself every day and when you're in any kind of situation that makes you feel self-conscious. One reader once told me that she mentally recites the line from *Almost Famous*: "I am a Golden Goddess." And then there's always "I so own this room."

SEVEN

15 Ways to Tap into
Your Inner Sex Kitten

O kay, so you know it's important to own your hotness, to appreciate how darn sexy you are. As I said, it's a *mental* strategy. But it's easier to acknowledge and appreciate your own sexiness if you regularly revel in it, if you choose to live a sensuous life. When you do sexy things, you just plain feel sexier. Try the following:

1. In warm weather (or cold if it moves you), walk around your home with no top on. Feel the breeze on your breasts.
2. Light candles around your place, but try them in exotic, woodsy scents rather than floral—they're so much more erotic. A fantastic one my beauty director turned me on to is Diptyque's Feu de Bois. You'll feel like a wood nymph when you smell it.
3. During dry spells in your dating life, wear sexy lingerie to bed.
4. Order or make yourself spaghetti *vongole* (spaghetti with clam sauce) and savor every bite. In fact, savor all of the food you eat by setting your utensils down between bites.
5. When you pleasure yourself, make it an experience— with great ambiance and good music.

6. If you can't afford sheets with really high thread count (600 feels like paradise), just buy the pillowcases.
7. Keep a bowl filled with tangerines on your table. They not only look great but they smell great, too.
8. Take deep breaths from your pelvis.
9. When you have a pedicure, ask for a ten-minute leg massage.
10. Lock eyes with cute guys on the street. Hold their gaze an extra beat.
11. Discover the fantastic cologne by Bobbi Brown called Beach. It smells like suntan lotion, the sea, and sexy summer sweat, and when you wear it, you feel as if you are lying on the beach in a bikini listening to the waves crash and feeling the sun on your body.
12. Have wine with lunch sometimes. In Provence, the French drink rosé with their lunch. It's a fantastic wine for summer.
13. Eat every meal you possibly can alfresco.
14. In winter, wear cashmere socks. Your feet will be in heaven.
15. Buy an overhead fan for your bedroom. When you sleep under it, you will feel as if you are in Jamaica.

EIGHT

When It Really Matters, Move *Fast*

I
f I assessed the many mistakes I've been guilty of at work
and in life over the years, most of them probably would involve making a stupid choice—based on lack of information or letting myself be swayed in the wrong direction (like when
years ago, at another magazine, I allowed an entertainment editor to talk me into putting a forty-something Warren Beatty on the
cover). But a few of my screwups fall into an entirely different
category: the I-didn't-take-*any*-action category—or I didn't take
action *fast* enough.

We've probably all hesitated to our own detriment on occasion. We become so busy or preoccupied that we don't respond
to a situation that's calling for action, or we don't know where to
start so we procrastinate until the situation works itself out without
us—and then we're not at all pleased with the results. We kick
ourselves for having failed to get off the dime quickly.

That's not to say there aren't occasions in life when it's essential to *pause*. Sometimes it really is better to hold off for a bit until
you have more information or you've cooled down. For instance,
when you're really pissed at someone and feel ready to tear the
top of her head off, it's almost always to your advantage to take
a chill pill. But I think more often than not, we rationalize not acting because we're uncertain how to proceed or we're paralyzed
with anxiety.

A couple of years ago I received a call saying that Goldie Hawn was making a movie about the editor of a women's magazine and she wanted to come to my office, along with a screenwriter, to interview me about how I performed my job. Would that be okay? *Duh, yes,* I wanted to yell into the phone. The experience turned out to be even more rewarding than I imagined. Goldie was down to earth and charming and very funny. At one point, while describing a turning point in her character's life—needless to say, she was going to be playing the editor in the movie—she did a hilarious imitation of a woman nearly howling in orgasmic pleasure. People on my staff were staring into my office with their mouths agape.

But here's the moment of that morning that I remember most. After the interview was over, Goldie walked over to my window and glanced out at the view down Fifty-seventh Street.

"Oh, I can see my apartment building from here," she said, pointing to a blue-gray high-rise half a block away. Though I knew she lived mainly on the West Coast, I'd read that she kept an apartment in Manhattan.

I joined her at the window.

"Then you're right across from our corporate headquarters," I said, referring to the landmark building the company owned. "You know, we're building a huge tower on the top of the original structure. It's going to be breathtaking."

She nodded politely and moved away from the window. I walked her and the screenwriter to the elevator, where they both said a gracious goodbye. Sometime later Goldie must have called a florist or had an assistant do it, because a beautiful orchid plant arrived with a lovely note from her.

That's not all she found the time to do that day. Exactly one week after our appointment, there was an item in the paper saying Goldie's New York apartment was on the market. Of course! I'd been so busy bragging about the new corporate tower it hadn't occurred to me that the tower would most likely block the view from her apartment! Perhaps it was all a coincidence. Regardless, within a few months, there was a follow-up item in the paper saying her place had sold for a sizable sum. I was awed by Goldie's apparent swiftness. Nothing in her charming, funky style had suggested that she could hightail it at the speed of a cheetah.

How do you learn to move that quickly in situations when being proactive can make a critical difference for you? I found a trick that works for me. I call it the "Do Just One Little Thing" strategy, which, depending on the circumstances, might mean making a phone call, shooting off an e-mail, or Googling a piece of info. This invariably leads to another little task and then, before I know it, I'm well into the process. It's like the first little wad of snow you gather in your mitten before you begin to roll a giant snowball.

Maybe that's how it worked for Goldie that day. I picture her grabbing her cell phone as soon as she hit the street and telling her assistant, "Find me a great real estate agent, *now.*"

PART TWO

YOU ON TOP

Work

NINE

How to Make an Awesome Impression

There are so many times in life when a killer impression can make all the difference. In job interviews, needless to say, but also when you're meeting your guy's parents or applying for a small-business loan or having a drink with someone you met online.

Unfortunately people can be fairly unforgiving when they meet you for the first time. There reportedly was once a study that determined that the decision not to hire is made within the first three minutes of a job interview. Yikes. You've barely had time to tell them that you've increased productivity by 15 percent.

I've thought a lot about first impressions, in part because I'm so often giving one but also because I meet new people regularly—not only job candidates but also experts and writers who are interested in becoming involved with the magazine somehow.

First of all, the surface, physical stuff really does matter. You can't help but take in the outfit, grooming, handshake, posture, eye contact, and even the bag and shoes. I know beauty is only skin deep, but like most people, I've been conditioned to believe that someone who is eager and worth dealing with makes an effort for the interview.

But there's something I think is just as key as a good handshake and a designer bag, and in the long run, more powerful: passion. When you're passionate—when you have energy and enthusiasm and a sense of commitment—people become instantly intrigued and even electrified by it.

Chances are if you are trying to make a good impression, there's something you're passionate about at that moment—such as securing the loan or getting his family to like you. The trick then is to just let it show. I have this sense that too often young women feel they have to be cool as a cucumber in that kind of a situation, and not give too much away. But I think it's the hot tamales who win the day, the ones who aren't afraid to wear their hearts (genuinely) on their sleeves.

Think about what the experience means for you—the chance to finally meet a guy you really enjoyed talking to online, for instance, or to work for a company with a great reputation—and let that feeling come through in your face and your words. It might be a matter of actually expressing how much you want what's on the table (like the loan) or letting your enthusiasm for the experience come through indirectly (which works well with guys)—as in "Thanks for picking this bar. I hear the apple martinis are fantastic here."

TEN

The 2 Things You Must Do in a New Job

I've handed out a whole bunch of promotions over the years, and it's interesting how individuals respond to them. Some people just flourish, even if they're terrified. Others, even those who are totally deserving of the promotion, flounder.

Though it's easy to feel frustrated with the flounderers, I also can relate to their situation. I know from experience how tough it is to walk into a brand new job and flawlessly pull it all together.

When you're stepping into a new job or promotion, you can make it easier if you tell yourself to just focus on two things: the mission and the message.

The Mission:
This is the work you need to do. It's amazing the number of people I've promoted who see the promotion as some kind of end point. It's as if they're thinking, *Whew, I did a really good job and got promoted.* They're not necessarily lazy but they don't think *forward* enough—about how their job has shifted and the new responsibilities they're supposed to be tackling. They keep doing the job they *used* to do. Or they want to do big things but they lose themselves in getting up to speed.

The key is to be certain of what your mission is—through conversations with your boss—and then set a course of action to accomplish it. Yes, you may need to engage in plenty of prep work, but I think it's also critical to come up with a strong innovation or concept fairly soon into your tenure, one that will dazzle your boss and prove you were a brilliant choice. I once heard a very successful woman sum it up this way: do one big thing and buy yourself some time.

The Message:
It would be nice if all you had to do was concentrate on the mission. But in a new job, you have to think of the message, too. And that message needs to move up and down the ladder—to your boss and to any people who report to you.

Your boss wants updates. He may seem laid back about it, but he's wondering what you're up to and if he made the right decision in hiring or promoting you. Shoot him e-mails, give reports, pop into his office.

If there are people working for you, you need to give them a sense of your plans. How are you going to change things? What will remain the same? What do you expect of them? Even if you are still slightly shell-shocked and unsure of exactly where you're headed, make a few announcements. It reinforces the idea that you *do* have a clue and eases their anxiety. As a friend of mine in the advertising business says, "People want to know what side of the boat they're supposed to row on." Initially you don't have to be too specific. People are surprisingly happy with generalities, like "I want this to be the department others turn to first," or "Let's review our commitment to creativity." If you don't tell them anything, they'll become restless. Not only will it be hard to convert them to your side down the road, but they will spread the word that you don't seem to know what you're doing.

ELEVEN

Sometimes You Have to Rent a Herd of Buffalo

I f I had to pick a particular lesson that sums up so much of what I've learned in the past eight years at *Cosmo*, it's this one: if you want to guarantee that something you do has a powerful impact, go out and rent a herd of buffalo.

That doesn't make much sense, of course, and I don't mean it literally. But it's the way I describe a certain approach to a situation, based on an experience I had with my photo director, Dennis Anderson, who started at *Cosmo* not long after me. He's extremely energetic and a perfectionist, a guy who prides himself on making sure everything is just right.

One day I dropped by Dennis's desk to see how arrangements were going for a fashion shoot in South Dakota. We were doing a story on clothes with a Native American feel, and South Dakota had seemed like the perfect location for the shoot.

"Everything's set," he told me. He explained that the location scout had found a beautiful area for the photographer to work in—with big sky and plenty of buttes rising in the background.

"Good," I said. "And maybe if we're lucky, a few buffalo will run by while he's taking his pictures."

He looked at me slightly stunned, almost offended.

"Well, I've *rented* a herd," he announced.

"You *rented* a herd?" I said. "Uh, wow. That's great." I meant it, though I was slightly blown away by his news. It hadn't occurred to me that you could just go out and rent an entire herd of buffalo.

"Oh, and by the way," he added. "They're the same herd that was used in *Dances with Wolves.*"

Not just any herd, I thought. *They have their SAG cards.*

Back in my office, I considered what Dennis had done. I liked that he'd been so incredibly proactive and had taken the extra step to make certain that the photos would be as awesome as possible. You could say he'd pumped the gas a few extra times, or in the words of Emeril Lagasse when he adds spice to a recipe on his cooking show, he'd kicked it up a notch. Rather than settle for good enough (buttes and big sky), he'd gone for the fab factor—big bruiser buffalo grazing in the background of the photographs.

I like to think I've always had a natural instinct to push things, to kick them up a notch, but hearing that phrase—"rent a herd of buffalo"—was great for me. It gave me a nice mantra to use every day. Because sometimes you get a little lazy or preoccupied, and the right mantra reminds you to push.

In certain instances you need the push to be a big one. The situation calls for something over the moon, something dazzling enough to make people gasp. Colin Cowie, the famous event designer who has arranged everything from Oprah's fiftieth birthday party to royal weddings in Qatar, told me he always aims for what he calls "jaw-dropping moments." In other words, after people walk into a room he's decorated for a party, they shouldn't be able to pick their jaws up off the floor.

That's exactly what he accomplished when we hired him the

first time at *Cosmo*. We were hosting a luncheon for four hundred people in order to salute the guys we'd picked as Fun Fearless Males—including Josh Duhamel, Kevin Bacon, and Benjamin McKenzie—and we wanted the room and the meal to be awesome. Colin didn't disappoint. The day of the luncheon the entire space was bathed in red light. The tablecloths were made of red, pink, and black Pucci-style fabric, and the centerpieces were huge balls of tightly packed red carnations. The appetizer was already set at each place and it played off the table decor. It was Caprese salad, but rather than the traditional slices of tomatoes and mozzarella, a whole tomato had been skinned to look like a red ball—just like the flowers—and then stuffed from the bottom up with mozzarella. Next to each plate in a slim shot glass was just the right amount of basil vinaigrette to pour onto the salad when you were ready to eat it. Okay, admittedly, a number of people mistakenly *drank* the vinaigrette that day, thinking the shot glasses held an *amuse-bouche*, but overall the whole effect was spectacular.

Going for the fab factor doesn't always require tons of effort, however—you don't have to skin four hundred tomatoes to have a powerful effect. I once heard a teacher tell one of my kids that the difference between a B+ and an A in a subject is ten minutes more of work a night. And that's often true with the difference between good enough and great. Sometimes it's just a little nudge, a few more minutes, an extra phone call (like the one to the buffalo wrangler). The tiniest thing can often deliver a big bang.

One of the designers we feature regularly in *Cosmo* is Kate Spade. She told me a very intriguing story once about how she got her start. She had decided to go into the handbag business and had designed a small group of bags. The night before she was going to present them at a trade show for buyers, she was sitting in her living room staring at them and realized that they were good enough but not *fantastic*. The biggest problem with them, she felt, was that there wasn't anything for the eye to go to. So she grabbed a pair of nail scissors, cut out all the black "Kate Spade New York" tags on the inside of the bags, and then hand sewed them to the outside of the bags. Okay, I think it's fair to say that the rest is history. I mean, Kate Spade's bags are amazing but if you had to describe the signature aspect of them, the iconic touch, it would be the black label on the outside that says "Kate Spade New York."

It must have been a bitch to sew on those tiny labels, but we're really just talking about one night of her life. And that made all the difference.

So whenever you're doing anything that you hope will impress people, seduce someone, or help you attain what you want, step back and ask yourself if you've gone as far as you can go. Or is there a way to push it, to kick it up a notch, or to *rent a herd of buffalo* so that it's even better? If the answer to the last question is yes, then go for it. It might make all the difference.

TWELVE

Don't Be Afraid to Be Kiss-Assy, but Do It in the Right Way

There have probably been times in life when you've wondered how much of a butt kisser you should be. You sensed in a particular situation that flattery or super friendliness was called for and might even give you an advantage. But you may have been reluctant to praise or ingratiate yourself for fear of coming across as disingenuous or unseemly or even pathetically obvious. Or you just may not see yourself as a bullshit artist.

But I have to say that, done right, butt kissing can be a good thing. It can encourage people to warm up to you and *does* help you snag what you want. (Hint: People like doing things for people who seem to like them!) Yes, you may be bullshitting a bit, but I don't think it's necessarily disingenuous, because the other person may very well see it for what it is. I once hired someone who was a hard-core butt kisser, and I know there were people on my staff who thought I was being completely snowed. But I not only saw through the butt kissing, I appreciated her behavior. She laid it on thick because she was passionate about her job and wanted to make sure I liked her. She was sometimes the one smiling face in a cluster of grumps. At the end of the day, I think a lot of us respect butt kissers for their enthusiasm and effort.

That said, you don't want to appear to be a total phony or ingrate. Here, the proper way to butt-kiss:

- When you decide to flatter, pick something to rave about that's fairly legitimate, even if you have to work hard to find it. Recently I interviewed a woman for a job who kept telling me, "Gosh, you're such a rock star." That rang about as true as someone telling me I had a real head for astrophysics. The only time I bear any resemblance to a rock star is when I'm wearing my phone headset.

  It's also smart to make your praise specific—it sounds more authentic that way. If you tell your boss, "Your speech was *brilliant*; I loved it," and he knows that half the audience was comatose, you *will* come across as a bullshit artist. But if you say something concrete like "I really related to that story you told about growing up in a small town," it sounds sincere.

- Maintain distance between ass kissing and solicitation. People will sometimes phone me, stroke me, and just as I am about to bask in the glow a teensy bit, they suddenly indicate the real reason for the call is that they are looking for a book agent and are hoping they can approach mine using my name or they need a letter of recommendation. Avoid this kind of twofer situation. It just looks so obvious. You want to allow for a gap between when you gush and when you ask. That's why it's good to make a habit of shooting people e-mails or dropping them notes the minute you hear about their accomplishments or good news. (Keep a stack of note cards near your desk with the envelopes already stamped.)

- Maintain ass-kissing speed. One flaw of many ass kissers is that they are all praisy upfront but as soon as they get a whiff that they're not going to get exactly what they want from you, they grind to a halt. For instance, I often receive e-mails from college grads saying how much they admire what I've accomplished and could they please arrange an exploratory interview with me. I e-mail them back, explaining that due to my schedule I am unable to conduct exploratory interviews, but I attach a file I've prepared on how to break into the magazine business. The vast majority of these women never write back to say thanks or acknowledge receiving the info. I get the feeling they are sitting at their computers thinking, *A fat lot of good my e-mail did me.* But by losing steam at the back end, they forfeit any chance of opportunity down the road, of me remembering them and possibly being able to do them a good turn later.

Every once in a while, though, there's an exception. Recently a senior named Katie from Duke University wrote asking me to speak at the school. My assistant explained to Katie that my schedule wouldn't allow for it despite how much I would have enjoyed going down there. Several weeks later I received a beautiful handwritten note from her saying she understood but just wanted to say how much I'd inspired her and that she had given my books to friends and relatives and that she hoped our paths would cross in the future.

I kept turning the note over hunting for the request for the favor, but there was none. *It was nothing more than a lovely note.* She had been as good at the back end as she was at the front end. Kate to Katie: *Wherever you are, I'll do almost anything for you. Just get in touch!!!*

THIRTEEN

You've Got to Drain the Swamp as You Slay the Alligators

Okay, you are probably sitting there wondering what the hell I mean by the title of this chapter. I will tell you but first let me say that I owe much success to this crazy-sounding gator game plan—not only in my job at *Cosmo* but also in both my personal life and my other "career" as a mystery writer.

I learned this strategy from a management guru when I was the editor in chief of a business magazine for women back in my thirties. It plays off the old expression "It's damn hard to drain the swamp when you're up to your ass in alligators." If you ponder that expression for a few seconds, you can probably relate to it. In life, we become so caught up in our day-to-day survival efforts (alligator slaying) that we don't have the time or energy to tackle the big, important stuff (swamp draining) that matters most in the long run.

The management guru's point, though, was that no matter how hard it may be, you *have* to find a way to work on the big stuff—developing your goals and your plan for accomplishing them. When you have a vision and strategy for bringing that vision to reality, it guarantees that what you *do* do on a day-to-day basis makes sense and moves you forward. For instance, once the swamp is drained, you won't even have to worry about those nasty alligators anymore.

Taking this strategy to *Cosmo* with me was critical in my being able to both survive and thrive. We're a magazine that must change constantly in order to meet the needs of a young, dynamic readership, and this big-picture thinking has to be an essential part of what I do each month. Yet it would be really easy for me to become distracted from that. There are a huge number of pages in each issue of *Cosmo*, almost double what many other magazines have, and just getting the magazine out the door every month is a bear of a job.

John Searles, my book editor and special projects director, told me a funny story that encapsulates how nutty it can become at *Cosmo*. He'd edited the excerpt of a sexy novel we were running and his assistant popped into his office and showed him that he'd written the following sentence, "With one hand Jack sipped his wine, with the other hand he stroked her thigh, and with the other hand he flipped the light switch."

What I've discovered is that the only way to ensure that I focus on the big picture is to *schedule* time to do so. Each month I block out an hour to analyze ratings and e-mails from readers and plot out how I might want to alter aspects of the magazine. I also schedule meetings with editors to discuss new columns, new features, and new directions. And often I just go out to a restaurant alone with a notepad and daydream about what road we should travel down next as a magazine.

And you know what? Most of our successful changes have come out of these private sessions or group planning meetings. A perfect example: About a year after I started, I realized from categorizing reader e-mails that one of the recurring themes was that readers wanted to see more sexy pictures of hunky guys. There might as well have been hordes of young women standing beneath my window shouting, "Kate, bring on the hot bodies—*now*!"

Because of that I decided to create a monthly portfolio of dreamy, partly-clothed guys, as well as a monthly column called "Guy Without His Shirt." One of my editors calls these our "hottie biscotti" pages, and readers adore them! But if I hadn't blocked out time to really analyze all the reader input, I might never have added these tantalizing naked male torsos to the mix.

When all hell is breaking loose on your job—because two of your co-workers are on maternity leave or the computers are down or your boss is hounding you for a sales report—focusing on "the future" may seem like a low priority, but it can ultimately save your ass, shape your destiny, and possibly lead to untold success.

But how do you make time for it if you *have* no time? Start with just thirty minutes once a month. Mark it on your calendar and consider it sacred. Once you see how helpful this kind of strategizing is, you'll want to do it more frequently. Just make certain it goes *on* the calendar. If you tell yourself that you'll just grab the minutes when you can, it won't happen.

I've also come to realize that it's great to use this strategy in your personal life, too. It's so easy to get caught up in the day-to-day grunt work—everything from grocery shopping to root canal appointments to mind-numbing runs to the dry cleaner—that you don't focus on your dreams and how to make sure they're going to unfurl. Taking a few minutes every week to step back, think, and plan allows you to do that.

I'll confess I never used the drain-the-swamp strategy when my kids were little. Because I was a working mom, I felt I shouldn't take a *second* away from my kids at night or on weekends. So I'd just plug away, slaying those alligators, trying to squeeze as much as I could into each twenty-four-hour period. Luckily I was able to leave work each day at five, but because my husband worked nights, I was on my own in the evening and often it felt positively nutty. I'd hurriedly change out of my work clothes, flinging them on the floor, play with my kids, sometimes run necessary errands with them, fix dinner, bathe them, play some more, read to them, and after they went to bed, I'd tackle a few hours of work (because I'd left at five!). My husband used to call just before ten to check in. I still remember a conversation we had one night when my son, our firstborn, was about eleven months old.

"How's it going?" he asked.

"Pretty good," I said. "I took Hudson out in the stroller and we ended up eating in a neighborhood restaurant. He's asleep now and I'm reading copy."

There was a long, odd pause.

"But his name is Hunter," my husband said finally.

Oops. That seemed to sum up just how overloaded I felt.

In hindsight, though, I wish I had taken a sliver of time each week to consider my big-picture goal (having a happy life as a working mom), because maybe it would have helped me rethink a few things and eliminate or delegate some tasks. Once my kids were older, however, I decided to apply the alligator-swamp strategy to my personal life and make time for musing about my life. I blocked out thirty minutes on the weekend to have a cup of coffee alone with nothing to do but think. And it was during one of these coffee klatches with myself that I decided that I was going to find a way to finally write a murder mystery.

So schedule time each week for planning, dreaming, and swamp draining. Is your life where you want it to be? If not, what do you need to do to get on track? Are you making time to smell the flowers? If not, what can you ditch to allow for it? Is there an old dream you want to resurrect? If so, what's the first step you could take toward it? And if things are really crazy, what could you do to bring your life a bit more under control?

If you come up with something fabulous you'd like to do and you wonder how you're going to find the time, see chapter 17 on delegating.

FOURTEEN

How to Spot a Rat at Work

S potting a rat can be tricky no matter where you are, but to me it always seems harder to do at work. You're spending all day with people, and yet you're witnessing them in only one domain of their lives, so you may not be totally clued in to who they are or what their true motives are.

But it's essential to be able to separate the good guys from the bad. If you don't, the bad ones can backstab you, undermine you, and even sabotage your success.

The very best lesson I know in sussing out office terrorists is one I learned after I'd been at *Cosmo* for about six months. I wish I'd learned it sooner—*years* sooner for that matter—but I've come to accept the fact it could only have dawned on me after a fair amount of trial and error.

Cosmo, when I arrived, seemed to have more than its share of troublemakers. I'm not sure why. Partly it had to do with the turmoil the place was in—the former editor in chief had departed without any warning, and people were worried about their future. Also, it had become a sort of cutthroat place to work, and that environment can not only bring out the worst in fairly nice people but also attract nasty types. Case in point: a month or two into my tenure, I decided to periodically invite guest speakers to our offices to share their stories with the staff in a "salon." Shoshanna Lonstein, former girlfriend of Jerry Seinfeld, was the first on my list. She had just started her own very charming clothing line, and I thought people would be interested in hearing her philosophy and strategies. The day after she stopped by, a very bitchy item about her visit ran on Page Six, the gossip page of the *New York Post*, claiming that during her talk she'd been sporting, God forbid, VPL—visible panty line. Some person on my staff had actually taken pleasure in placing that mean little item.

Several incidents like that proved the rats were there, but rooting them out turned out to be harder than I imagined. For one thing, there seemed to be so many varieties. I was dealing not only with straight-out nasty stuff from some individuals, but also with guerrilla tactics from others, as well as that old workplace favorite—passive-aggressive behavior. I also sensed that one or two of the nicest *seeming* people might actually be dangerous. For instance, there was this one chick—I'll call her Pam—who was effusively helpful to me from the start. She said she'd been invited to follow the other editor in chief to her new gig but in the end had decided to stay and was looking forward to working with me and having more responsibility. She also told me that there were several freaked-out staffers in her department, and that she would be happy to work with them directly. They were suspicious of me as the new boss, she said, but were tight with her—and she could cool them down and convince them to stay. Despite the air of cooperation, I picked up a bad vibe from her.

I spent a lot of time trying to analyze the different people I thought might be rats, waiting for them to finally show their hands—or teeth. In some instances I even gave people the benefit of the doubt because it seemed unfair *not* to—at least until I had evidence.

Eventually the troublemakers did reveal themselves, but in

hindsight I realized that I'd wasted valuable time and energy. I'd been trying to identify what *kind* of rat each one was and then find actual proof—for instance, catch the suspected backstabbers red-handed and the smiley ones doing something obviously two-faced.

But here's the lesson that finally sunk in for me: when you are trying to root out suspected rats, you don't need to figure out what *type* they are or wait until you catch them rifling through your drawers or phoning in a VPL exposé to Page Six. You just have to do one thing: notice how you *feel* when you're around them. Because people who are rats almost always make you feel uncomfortable. You don't need proof, you don't need to catch the rat red-handed. Your subconscious is already picking up on a ton of clues and telling you everything you need to know.

For instance, I was *always* uneasy around Pam. She'd offer me these big smiles and sugary tones, but after she trotted out of my office, my stomach invariably felt as if my assistant had just stepped into the room and announced, "The FBI is on the phone for you—they say it's urgent." Pam left for another job eventually, and the sensation that overwhelmed me immediately after her departure was relief.

So note how you feel when you're around someone who might be trouble. Does your stomach churn? Is your pulse racing? Do your cheeks ache from fake smiling? That's all the evidence you need that there is something wrong. From that point on, do not let your guard down, and watch the person like a hawk. If you're in a position to remove them from your presence—because you're the boss—do it swiftly. Of course, before you take drastic action like that, you're going to want to verify your feelings, but that will be easier to do now that you've accepted that you have a problem on your hands. One great way to flush out a rat is to ask him or her lots of direct questions. Many baddies tend to squirm when they suspect you are on to them. This question strategy probably would have worked perfectly on Pam. I later found out that the people she said were her little pets couldn't stand her, and that she had told one of my favorite staffers I didn't like her but that she, Pam, was going to be her protector. Pam was simply on a power trip. If I had really pressed her with questions about each of these people, she probably would have squirmed enough for me to know she was lying.

And what if the person is a peer and you can't get rid of her or him? Distance yourself as much as possible. Avoid team projects and any kind of socializing. If the person is in meetings with you and has a tendency, as rats do, to co-opt other people's ideas, you might want to submit your ideas to your boss in writing. You should also get as much face time with your boss as possible so he or she sees your true worth. And when you have to interact with a rat, do as much as possible by e-mail so there's always a paper trail.

FIFTEEN

Be There First

For most of my life, I was a total night owl. I liked to stay up late reading, finishing up work I wasn't able to complete during the day, sometimes just puttering or taking a long bubble bath. I practically needed to be beaten with a rubber hose to get out of bed in the morning. (My husband claims I've set a world record with the number of times I've slapped the snooze button on my clock radio.) I used to force myself to go into work at a *relatively* decent hour, but I was never ahead of the pack.

Once my kids started attending school, I altered my schedule so I could drop them off on the way to work, and that meant dragging myself out of bed at an ungodly hour for me. And when I began at *Cosmo*, I decided to make another shift. I woke up even earlier, took the kids to school a bit earlier, and didn't linger in the classroom anymore. With the volume of work my new job presented, I realized that for a certain stretch in my life I was going to have to be both a night owl *and* an early bird. (Granted, this is also called burning the candle at both ends, but I try not to think about it that way.)

A funny thing happened as soon as I made the switch. I discovered that even though it was tough for me to crawl out of bed, I really liked being among the first ones to show at work every day. I realized that it gives you a chance to catch your breath, tidy your desk, delete overnight spam, and, most important, collect your thoughts. When the day starts hurtling along, you're already in a nice groove. I only wished that I'd discovered years earlier the great advantage that *early* and *first* offered.

It works with meetings and appointments, too. At the very least, making sure you're not late prevents you from losing a certain edge. A couple of months ago I got my signals crossed about a meeting outside of the office and showed up fifteen minutes late. Even though no one seemed to mind, I felt as though I never eased into the flow of the meeting—I was always in this mental catch-up mode. Later I discovered that because so many people had been late, the meeting had actually started only a couple of minutes before I made it and I hadn't missed anything of significance. My only real disadvantage had been the rattled feeling. You can practically never shake it if you've arrived late.

So even if it's not in your constitution to be an early bird, just try it for a stretch. You'll discover that when you're there first, you seem to stay on track better. If it's too torturous to get up earlier every day, doing it even once in a while will give you an edge. As for appointments, all you have to do to guarantee that you'll be early is to subtract real (I said *real*) travel time from the moment you need to arrive and then leave about seven minutes prior to that. That should give you the padding you require.

SIXTEEN

Yes, You Need to Sweat the Small Stuff

One of the best strategies you can use in business is to stay as focused as possible on the most significant projects and not become mired in inconsequential minutiae. The dumb little stuff is not only a time suck, but it's an energy suck as well. You can usually delegate it or skip it altogether. Someone on my staff once worked for a woman who makes her editors explain each of their editing changes in the margin of the page. I'm sure that editor in chief believes she is being amazingly thorough and conscientious by demanding all that commentary, but I couldn't help but think how much smarter it is to just decide whether or not you *like* an editor's changes and, if you do, go with them without bothering to hear the explanations—and use all that extra time you have to develop big, bold new ideas for the magazine. I try never to get bogged down in trivia.

Having said that, I've come to see that there is sometimes merit in sweating the small stuff—if it has the potential to open your eyes or lead to an awesome idea. When you take a closer look at a situation or plumb deeper for more information, you may discover a nugget that can be leveraged for enormous opportunity.

One thing I like to do when I get a chance, for instance, is to read the backup research on articles we're doing. Not because I don't trust my editors but because I'll often find a tangential detail that will spark an idea for an entirely different article. We do reader surveys and I never let myself just skim them. I analyze the results on the computer and look for new or unexpected patterns that could be addressed. I know I'm probably infamous for going off on tangents in meetings, but when I hear an anecdote or fact that catches my fancy, I like to stay with it for a while, working it over in my brain to see where it takes me.

I came up with one of my all-time favorite ideas that way. At one of our twice-weekly photo meetings, we were discussing a shoot for "Guy Without His Shirt," a monthly feature I introduced four or five years ago because so many readers were clamoring for male eye candy. During our discussion that day, I suddenly reflected on an extended version of this feature we'd done two years earlier, in which we'd sent model/actor Will Toale out and about through New York without his shirt and photographed his journey. It was hilarious, and I said we should find a reason to send another shirtless guy out on the town. A few minutes later we were discussing an upcoming article called "The Male Brain, Explained." We decided to shoot a woman as a scientist examining a guy with electrodes on his scalp. My photo director, Dennis Anderson, laughed and said, "We should have the guy lying there without his shirt."

I smiled at his suggestion and let my mind ramble. And then, in a flash, I had a brainstorm. "Why don't we do an *entire issue* in which every guy is shirtless?" I asked. We picked the March 2006 issue for our project and it was one of the most fun projects we've undertaken at *Cosmo*: In every photo or illustration featuring a male (whether celeb, model, or real guy), he was shirtless. We even included a photo of a little Boston terrier in pants and no shirt. I never would have come up with the concept if I hadn't been sweating the small stuff.

So as important as the big details are, don't allow yourself to be so caught up in them that you lose sight of little things that might have unforeseen potential. It's kind of like mining for gold. Tedious at times, not always productive, but occasionally a bonanza—which in the long run can help you with the big stuff.

Let's say, for instance, that you're in sales and one day you see an uptick on your progress chart indicating that a chunk of business came from a certain area. Rather than simply note it and pat yourself on the back for a good effort, ask yourself if there's something about that area that you should be paying attention to. Is it a particularly ripe territory? Should you be putting more of your effort there? Is there a way to take what you're doing in that location and do it elsewhere? It's also something you can use in your personal life. Do you always find yourself perusing nature books at the bookstore? Could it mean you're a city girl longing for more of the out-of-doors?

So, yes, keep your eye on the big picture, but don't be blind to good stuff that comes in small packages. If one small detail grabs your attention, stay with it and ask yourself why. Is there a meaningful aspect there, something worth learning more about or leveraging to your advantage?

SEVENTEEN

5 Little Tricks to Delegating

I don't have to tell you the advantage of delegating. We've all experienced the sheer pleasure that comes from relieving ourselves of stuff we're too busy to handle. Plus, common wisdom holds that high achievers are master delegaters.

But though we're aware of how essential delegating is, we're often dumb about it. We keep doing things we'd be better off relinquishing, because we don't know how to get rid of them or because there doesn't seem to be anyone to unload them onto or because we're afraid that if we pass them along, the other person will botch the job. This holds true both at work and in our personal lives.

I've always had a tough time balancing my need to micromanage with the awareness that my schedule just can't tolerate *everything*. But I've been forced to be a decent delegater because both my job and my personal life have become busier in recent years. I'm still learning in this arena, but here's what I've figured out so far:

1. If you dread it, dump it—or at least do your best to. If you're stuck with something you can't stand, then it's not only making you miserable but it's also sucking valuable energy out of your life. Marcus Buckingham, a motivational speaker and author (*The One Thing You Need to*

Know) who we often interview for *Cosmo*, told me that one of the secrets of very successful people is that they spend more time doing what they love than people who *aren't* successful. And you can't be doing things you love if you're stuck doing things you don't love.

2. So how do you unload a job you abhor or just don't have time for? One trick is to simply stop doing it without even bothering to delegate it. Some tasks, you see, turn out to be unnecessary—like sending Christmas cards perhaps. I figured that out with certain meetings. I need to brain-storm with people in my job but I find that *big* meetings are generally unproductive (because they drag on inter-minably and also people in large groups tend to be less forthcoming about what they really think). I also dread seeing my calendar eaten up by meetings. So now when I have a matter to share or discuss, rather than having my assistant schedule a get-together, I might do a drive-by—I'll stop by a particular editor's office, perhaps even pull someone else in with me, and quickly relay my thoughts or ask for insight. Then I'll ask that editor to fill in anyone who needs to be in the loop. These meetings take five minutes instead of thirty.

   There are certain jobs that just can't be eliminated, so then you must dump them on another person. There's al-most always a person you can give a task to if you sweeten it enough. Sweetness, of course, can be in the form of money (if you don't have it, try bartering), but also it could be praise, or the respect that comes from more responsibility, or access.

3. Even if you're afraid to let go of a task because another

person won't do it as well as you, try it just *once*. What you discover when you delegate is that you are often able to settle for good enough. A couple of years ago I hired a college student to help me with a ton of personal tasks, everything from making household purchases to researching vacations on the Internet. At first I was anxious about delegating so much. For instance, if she was scouring the Web for a new kitchen clock for me, how would I know she'd found all the options? But over time I saw that it didn't really matter if I saw every clock imaginable. If I found one I liked among those she forwarded to me, then that was good enough.

4. Women often find it hard to delegate to their guy because they're afraid he will not do the job, do it poorly, or bristle at the request. But guys *will* respond if you communicate effectively. The trick is to be clear and concise, something I've stressed elsewhere in this book. Don't use broad, vague statements like "I need you to *do* more when we have people over." Say instead, "Tonight can you please be in charge of getting people drinks."

5. Regularly reconsider. Here's the most important secret I've ever learned about delegating, and it came from a successful woman I interviewed. You can't just decide once what you should let go of. Periodically review your to-do list and knock items off. Too often we take on new jobs and projects without thinking about how to let go of something else in order to have balance. Once every few weeks ask yourself if there's anything you've started dreading. If there is, reread 1 through 4.

EIGHTEEN

People Who Act
All Innocent Rarely Are

This isn't one of those lessons that's going to change your life, but I learned it a few years ago, and I think it can be useful when you're trying to evaluate what someone is up to.

For many years we had a columnist who was quite popular with readers. However, very gradually—but inexorably—the reader ratings of the column began to decline. We did several analyses and devised a few fix-it strategies, but nothing halted the decline. Eventually the writer's contract came up for renewal. Because we had a long-standing relationship with this person, we didn't want to just bag her column. So I suggested that the editor, John Searles, have a candid discussion with her and share our concerns. Maybe she would have insight about what to do. In her column she frequently advised the use of honesty, and I thought that tactic would work best with her.

John told me that she handled the news well. She said she had a few ideas on how we could kick life into the column, and she agreed to work on a monthly contract until we had a clearer vision for the future. The ratings improved but unfortunately only marginally. About nine months into this arrangement, the columnist suddenly e-mailed John and me and told us that she had decided to move on. She said she didn't want to write this type of column anymore.

I felt bad. I wondered if the columnist hadn't been as comfortable with the new arrangement as she'd seemed. Here was my chance to drop the column without having to actually fire her, and yet I just felt too much loyalty to her. I told John to switch gears, to give her a yearlong contract and make one last stab at jump-starting the ratings.

When John e-mailed her with this game plan, she suggested that he work out the arrangements with her agent. "I let my agent handle contract stuff," she told him. "I don't really know anything about these things." There were several other e-mail exchanges, in which she kept stressing how ignorant she was about contract matters. Then suddenly she e-mailed to say that she was going to be doing a column for another magazine and would no longer be writing for us. It turned out that she had been offered the arrangement several months before—and the "I'm clueless" e-mails had been her way of buying time while she worked out the details.

John and I just had to roll our eyes when the whole thing was over. Of course, you couldn't blame the writer for the move. She knew her situation with us was imperiled, and God bless her, she'd scored another deal for herself. Eventually we brought in another writer and the new column now rates significantly higher than the old one.

What kept bugging me, however, was how we'd been strung along. In her column the writer had used statements like "The key is to talk calmly, honestly, and openly," and yet she had not done so with us. I was especially annoyed that we hadn't seen what was coming. I asked John what his final assessment of the situation was and whether he thought there was any take-away for us, any lessons to be learned.

"There's definitely a lesson here," he said. "You know how she kept pretending to be real innocent about the whole contract situation and kept telling us to deal with the agent? It made me realize that anyone who makes a big deal of how innocent she is probably isn't."

I think he nailed it. As I mulled over his words, I realized that the lesson applied to other situations I'd found myself in over the years.

People who act all innocent and dumb about what's going on rarely are. Be wary of phrases like "Gee, I really don't know," "I haven't a clue," and "I'll have to get back to you on that."

NINETEEN

There *Is* Such a Thing as Career Karma

Not long after I arrived at *Cosmo*, we received an e-mail from a young woman bemoaning the fact that she was in love with a married man who *really, really* cared about her but didn't seem at all inclined to leave his wife for her. We're frequently e-mailed by readers asking for advice, but there was a twist at the end of this one. The woman named her lover and he turned out to be a familiar name in the magazine business. The editor who first perused the e-mail forwarded it to another editor, thinking she'd get a kick out of it since she'd once worked with the guy and wasn't a fan of his. That woman immediately—and smugly—sent it to as many people as she could think of.

After hearing about the incident, I called this editor into my office for a confab. I believe I started our discussion with a phase along the lines of "What in God's name were you *thinking*?" I told her that her behavior was childish and beneath someone in her position (she's since moved on to another magazine, by the way). "At the very least," I finally blurted out, bewildered by her actions, "you ought to consider what something like this does to your career karma."

Until that phrase popped out of my mouth, I don't think I'd actually formed it in my mind. But there really is such a thing as career karma. In the world of work, what goes around comes around. If you are good to a co-worker, there may come a time down the road when that person will look out for your welfare or perform a favor on your behalf. If you're nasty, however, she may find a way to retaliate—for instance, trashing you to others. People tend to have long, elephant-like memories when it comes to work—about both the good stuff and the bad. Perhaps it's because truly generous deeds aren't always expected and therefore leave a positive lasting impression. And maybe we remember evil deeds because there's often little opportunity to respond effectively at the time, which encourages us to stew and even nurse revenge fantasies.

You have to decide on your own code of conduct for your job, and I'm not going to preach. But at the very least, keep the karma concept in mind. It may involve a short-term sacrifice to take the high road, but it can pay off big for you later.

Here's a confession about myself and career karma. Several years ago I arranged for us to feature Ashlee Simpson on the cover. She hadn't been on any major magazine covers yet, but I knew our readers were snapping up her newest CD and were probably very curious about her. The moment just seemed right. Well, shortly before we were set to shoot the cover, Ashlee performed on *Saturday Night Live* and got caught lip-synching. There was a ton of flak about it in the media, and suddenly an evil thought flashed through my mind: *Is there any way I can get out of this?* The situation I found myself in certainly didn't rank up there with my worst experience with cover-timing (that occurred while I was editing *McCall's*, when two weeks before our cover story on the happy marriage of Michael Douglas and his then-wife Diana was due to hit newsstands, Douglas checked into a clinic for a reported sex addiction). But I still was worried that the Ashlee issue would bomb.

Though my initial instinct was to bail, in the end I couldn't do it. I'd given her publicist my word and he was one of the good guys. Plus, I still thought Ashlee was adorable and worthy of a cover. And lastly, I was afraid of what would happen to my career karma if I went back on my word.

To help guard against disaster, I decided to make the cover as dazzling as possible, adding plenty of bells and whistles. My design director and I decided we'd shoot Ashlee in an awesome red dress and use a white background so the red dress really popped. The fashion director called in a zillion red dresses, and the design director even ordered a different paper stock for the cover so that the white background would be really white. My executive editor, Michele Promaulayko, and I worked for hours on the coverlines, trying to make them tantalizing. I thought the one we came up with about Ashlee was especially compelling: "Don't Judge Her Till You Read This."

Well, guess what? The issue ended up being the best selling February cover in over a decade. And in the end I don't think it was due all that much to the bells and whistles we added but more to Ashlee's popularity and, yes, somewhat to the controversy surrounding her. Shortly after we went on sale, I heard that another magazine backed out of a cover with her, claiming that they hadn't known about *our* cover—though it was pretty obvious that we'd simply provided a convenient excuse for them. I wondered if they kicked themselves when they later saw our sales numbers. I was just delighted that my fear of bad karma had guided me into making the right call.

Here are a few ways to safeguard your own career karma:

- Do not bad-mouth people. It can be tough because certain people are so *deserving*, but if you find yourself being led into a bash fest, force yourself to listen rather than talk. If others look to you for reinforcement of their cattiness, you can shrug your shoulders, roll your eyes, or shake your head in bewilderment rather than say anything.

- Never ever break a confidence. Practically no one seems to keep a secret anymore, and so anyone who tells you one hoping that you'll suddenly staple your lips together is pretty stupid. But regardless, he or she will be unforgiving if you tell. To learn how to keep a secret, see chapter 80.

- Always thank a person who has done you a good turn. Not just with an e-mail either. Certain good turns are big enough to call for a handwritten note, flowers, or even a gift. It's always fascinating to me to see who sends a note and who doesn't. I gave a very expensive dinner party in honor of a well-known actress at a restaurant in Manhattan — to help her promote her special project — and didn't even receive an e-mail from her afterwards. But after a large party for *Cosmo*, when I'd never even expected any follow-up, Tony Danza sent a handwritten note thanking me. I try not to hold a no-note experience against anyone because we all become busy, but it can't help but put a damper on your enthusiasm to do anything else for the person.

- If you are going to have to do something unpleasant to another human being, consider at least warning the person (if it's appropriate). People hate the surprise element of bad things almost as much as the bad thing itself. It's not uncommon for some women's magazines to do unauthorized covers on celebrities, and that drives publicists insane. But my entertainment director, a former publicist herself, says that the reaction is often less negative if the publicist is warned in advance. Let's say that you are aware that a good friend of yours has been approached about a job and you get called in for an interview at the same spot. You may convince yourself that it's best not to say anything upfront. But think of how she'll feel if she learns that you landed the job when she never even knew you were a candidate. Forewarn her. It may piss her off if you do indeed land the job, but at least you were straight with her and you stand a chance of being forgiven.

- Find reasons to compliment your co-workers' performance to other people, including superiors. Not only does it help them, but it makes you look good, too.

- After you leave a job, never bad-mouth people in your former company no matter how stinky they were. You may want to work there again someday, despite how hard it is to imagine that *now*. It's also very bad to complain about an evil boss when you are in a job interview, even if the mood is easy and chatty or the interviewer is pressing you. She's really just fishing for info, and if you dish, it will end up reflecting badly on *you*. Say something that has a ring of authenticity but isn't negative—such as "I know people say he's tough but I learned an awful lot from him."

- And never ever say anything nasty in an e-mail! It lives on forever!

TWENTY

3 Secrets to Getting a Golden Gut

I'm sure there have been more than a few times in your life when you were about to make a decision and a friend told you, "Just listen to your gut." Our gut is supposed to be this marvelous tool that if used correctly helps us ignore all the extraneous noise and make the right call in a situation—almost by *feeling* rather than by thinking. My famous predecessor, Helen Gurley Brown, has admitted that she made *Cosmo* a huge success by simply listening to her gut—and never doing a lick of research.

But as much as we hear about the value of listening to our gut, some of us don't know what that involves. How are we supposed to know when it's talking to us? And how do we know what it's trying to say?

This really became a concern for me at *Cosmo*, not only because I had to make creative decisions at a faster clip than ever, but also because there was so much at stake with those decisions. More than ever, I wanted to be able to rely on my gut. Well, I read lots on the subject and experimented regularly, and though my gut may not be 14K, it's much better than it used to be. Here are the three best tricks I learned.

1. **If you feel something, it means something.** The trick is to acknowledge the vibe you're experiencing and stay with

it for a while. What does it seem to be telling you? Why are you suddenly experiencing it *now*? Often, if you're feeling something, others are as well. The first time I saw an episode of *Grey's Anatomy*, I was hooked and I thought Patrick Dempsey was about as hot as a blow-torch. So I said let's make him our Fun Fearless Male of the Year. I didn't ask a zillion other women what they thought, because I just had this sense that my reaction was so strong, it had to be pretty universal. It turned out that a ton of women were gaga about him and the show.

Richard Spencer, the very talented editor of the celebrity magazine *In Touch*, told me that he encourages editors to go with stories on the topics that appeal to them, because those are usually the ones everyone else wants to know about, too.

Sometimes the vibe you're getting is negative. Let's say your boyfriend sounded very odd on the phone and it made your tummy churn. Has he ever sounded like that in the past? When he was upset? Guilty? Is the feeling you're experiencing *worry*? As I said, your feelings generally mean something so don't ignore them.

2. **Watch for patterns.** Jane Buckingham, a *Cosmo* contributing editor and the head of the Intelligence Group, a research and trend-spotting organization, says that people tend to dismiss what's called "grandma" or "mother-in-law" research, which basically means that a certain piece of info keeps popping up anecdotally. But Buckingham sees value in that kind of pattern. "In my company we say that, if three people are doing it, it's a sign that it may be an emerging trend," says Buckingham. "Of

course it's not scientific but it means it's time to pay attention."

So when you hear or see something more than once, consider whether there's a "trend" happening and whether it's meaningful. It's a little like playing connect the dots. Did someone share a far-fetched sounding rumor that your company was in financial trouble and then you overheard someone else talking about bills not being paid? Those are two dots worth connecting. Did your boyfriend, who never works late, suddenly have to work until nine one night last week—and then again this week? When dots connect, it's time to ask a few questions and investigate.

3. **Trust your gut but teach it first.** It would be great if we could just look at a situation and instinctively have this perfect sense about it. But most of us can't do that in a vacuum—we need information. The more information you provide to your gut, the more accurate its response will be.

Not long after I arrived at *Cosmo*, I was trying to decide between two covers for a particular issue and I couldn't make up my mind. In desperation, I had photocopies of the two photos mounted onto boards and I took them to a shopping mall. I approached women, introduced myself, and asked them to help me choose. I am sure these women thought I had escaped from an insane asylum and was pretending to be the editor of *Cosmo*, but after eyeing me warily, most made a choice for me.

I ended up going with the one the majority chose, which was my favorite, too, and I'll never actually know if the other one would have sold better. But here's the fascinating discovery I made. Almost without exception, the women I interviewed asked me, "Which month is this for?" before choosing. And I saw for the first time the importance of the seasonality of the clothes the model was wearing. In general, *Cosmo* covers have a sort of timeless quality, and yet it was clear that women wanted the clothes to make sense for the season. I would never have known that if I hadn't done the research.

You don't want to overload your gut with info that isn't relevant, but wherever possible, provide it with facts that can help you with your choice. And when your gut instinct runs contrary to your research? Buckingham says to go back and do even *more* research. Keep digging for the answer.

TWENTY-ONE

How to Come Up with a Killer Idea

One of the things I'm obsessed about, as both an editor and a mystery writer, is ideas. Where do they come from and how do you guarantee a steady stream of good ones? Because I believe that a magazine needs to constantly evolve, I'm always on the lookout for ideas to improve *Cosmo*. But I also write a murder mystery each year, and that means I must generate ideas in that domain as well. In one day I might have to create a new fashion or relationship column but also come up with a delicious way to kill someone off.

A fascinating aspect of creativity is that ideas often pop into your brain from out of the blue for no apparent reason (of course there *is* a reason but you may not figure it out). It can be a magical experience, especially after you've considered or studied that idea for a day or two and realize that it's actually a winner.

But as magical as this "popping" thing is, you can't always wait for it to happen. You may need your idea *now*, thanks to a deadline or the fact that everyone is depending on it. At such moments it's easy to feel panicky. And that's why my quest has always been to figure out how to make good ideas pop up *on demand*. Over time I've found something that works for me, and in recent years I've relied on it constantly. It goes basically like this: *When you need a killer idea, you must leave home and take the question with you.* In other words, you've got to form what you're looking for into a question and then head out into the world to allow the answer to be presented to you.

I know that sounds hopelessly New Agey, but I'm not really the New Agey type (with the exception of loving hot stone massages). As a matter of fact, I think this technique works for a very obvious reason: *ideas have to be sparked and something has to spark them.* Sure, good ideas can be triggered from thoughts and memories floating around in your brain, but sometimes what's up there seems to be nothing but the same old stuff. If you haul yourself out into the world, there's lots of *new* stuff to inspire you. (This is not unlike what I said in chapter 1 about figuring out what you want to do in life.) You can snag ideas from movies, plays, art exhibits, billboards, street fashion, snippets of overheard conversations, menus, cartoons, sunsets, and so on and so on. Lionel Bart, the man who wrote the musical *Oliver*, admitted that the idea was sparked for him from seeing a candy bar called Oliver with the phrase "Please, sir, I want some more" printed on the wrapper. Bobbi Brown, the head of Bobbi Brown cosmetics, says she came up with the idea for her Slopes makeup line from seeing the white skin and rosy cheeks of people as they came off the chairlift in Aspen. I picked up the idea for setting my second mystery, *A Body to Die For*, in a spa from staring at the cold, steely equipment during a facial.

And why, once you go out into the world, do you need to form your quest into a question? I don't know for sure. But it really seems to work. It's as if you are priming your brain to be receptive. At a conference I took part in, the legendary dance choreographer Twyla Tharp, author of *The Creative Habit: Learn It and Use It for Life*, said posing the question is critical for her, too.

Whenever I'm stuck and can't generate an idea, I just take my question and *go*. The farthest afield I've ever traveled for an answer is London. Not long ago I was feeling ready to kick things up a bit with *Cosmo*, and I decided to go on the road with a question. Two years before, I'd totally rearranged the magazine based on the format of many European magazines. In the U.S., women's magazines have traditionally had an eclectic mix of short pieces in the front and then a mix of longer pieces in the back. European magazines just start off with a bang, with lots of splashy pieces, and they tend to organize features by category. To me, that approach made perfect sense for busy young women—and I rearranged *Cosmo* that way. Readers loved it.

Because that idea had come to me in London, I thought I'd give London another try. It just so happened that I was going to a murder mystery conference in Oxford for a weekend in August, so I decided to add a day to my journey and see what I came up with. I arrived in London at about 10 a.m., dropped my bags off at the hotel, and left with my question in my brain: *What's the next big thing I should do with* Cosmo?

I started off by just roaming down those wonderful London streets and alleys. After lunch, I wandered through Hyde Park. It was a warm, cloudless day, and people were everywhere. I stopped in a gallery, as well as the Victoria and Albert Museum. After a nap at my hotel, I went back out and again strolled along the streets. I ate dinner alone, very late. It was an enchanting day—but no answer came to me.

I didn't panic. I just put my question aside for the time being, and the next morning I headed to my mystery conference. It was interesting but a bit stiff (should you use that word about a murder mystery conference?). The average age of the participants was at least sixty-something, and I half expected one of the participants to start telling stories about the Blitz. I was surprised, then, one night to find someone sitting across the dinner table from me who was nineteen. Her mother had come to the conference, and since she was a student nearby, she tagged along. I began talking to her about her favorite magazines and then, *boom*, she said something that was a eureka moment for me. Her words triggered a brainstorm, and I knew immediately what I was going to do with *Cosmo*.

So that's what works for me—taking my question out into the world. And the nice thing is it's given me an excuse to visit London every year.

TWENTY-TWO

The One Sure Way to Be Famous

A few months ago I was making a television appearance, and while leaving the studio greenroom, I bumped into a well-known model I'd met on several occasions. She was there to promote a big project and after she described it to me, I asked if she was managing to squeeze in any modeling.

"Not these days," she said. "I'm really a *brand* now."

I almost burst out laughing, but then I couldn't really blame her for speaking in those terms because career experts and magazines like *Fast Company* tell us we need to brand ourselves today. It seems a little silly to go through life viewing yourself as comparable to Tropicana orange juice or Bounty paper towels, but it does pay to develop a great reputation. When there's buzz about you, people start coming to *you*.

It can take years to develop a great reputation, but there is a way to jump-start the process. The strategy is summed up beautifully by a woman I know who runs a very successful company. "The secret," she says, "is to do *one or two things* really well." And make sure everyone knows it.

I remembered this recently when my executive editor and I created a new position for someone already on staff. When I think of this person there are two things that just leap out: she writes dazzling copy and she always gets her work in on time. It's a killer combo.

So figure out one or two concrete things you want to be known for. Some possibilities:

- Listening really well
- Having an apartment that people love to hang at
- Being a great public speaker
- Organizing things brilliantly
- Staying calm in a crisis
- Making the best martinis on the planet

Take on projects that allow you to showcase those qualities even more. And don't be afraid to advertise them. Say things like "I'd be glad to do that. I'm a nut for organization," or "I make a mean martini."

PART THREE

YOU ON TOP

Men and Love

TWENTY-THREE

Your Guy Will Never Ever Be Like You

There was a period of time not all that long ago when it seemed that women believed that the world would be a better place if guys would just act the way females do. Relationships would run more smoothly and couples would bond tighter if guys could only learn to listen more, chat more, and also become more sensitive and romantic. It also seemed that many women believed—and were encouraged to believe by some pop psychologists—that if they worked hard enough at it, they could *teach* men to be more chick-like.

But if there is one thing I am sure of after eight years at *Cosmo*, it is that no matter how much you try to train a guy or how much white wine you serve him, he will not develop female instincts. After reading thousands of comments and e-mails from guys, I am struck by their immutable guyness. Most men you meet will never:

1. Talk as much as you do.
2. Ask questions as much as you do.
3. Love long, languorous, romantic dinners.
4. Feel an urge to discuss how beautiful the sunset is.
5. Be the first to say "I'm sorry."
6. Go step by step with you while you worry a situation to death.

7. Stop saying "Whatever *you* want to do" when you ask them what they feel like doing tonight.
8. Listen intently as you describe how annoyed you are with your mother, sister, sister-in-law, best friend Becky, or the girl who sits two cubes away from you at work and punctuates her phone conversations every four seconds with the word "Perfect."
9. Want to cuddle sometimes *instead* of having sex.
10. And so on.

Rather than be discouraged by this information, I think women should find it reassuring. When you're frustrated in certain situations because you can't connect with your guy, you can tell yourself that it doesn't reflect shortcomings on your part but rather just a dissimilarity in wiring. And despite all the differences, you certainly can help a man appreciate your approach to life and even convince him to adjust his behavior at times so it doesn't work your last nerve. I offer advice on doing that in a bunch of chapters.

But there's something else you might want to consider. The more I've listened to guys' words and gotten a handle on their guyness, the more I've found that some of their tactics are worth emulating. We often tend to view guy behavior as deficient and sigh-worthy, and yet I think there's a lot to be learned from it. Experiment a bit and give the guy approach a try from time to time. It may not come naturally but if you stay with it, I think you'll find that certain behavior has real value. A few suggestions:

- If you're out to dinner with your guy and you're the one who always drives the conversation, see what it's like not to talk every minute and just flow with the silences. Try letting him raise conversation topics. There may be occasional gaps, but it will be fascinating to see where he leads the discussion.

- The next time you're about to plan one of your hopefully romantic Friday or Saturday night dinners with your guy, opt instead for an activity that's very guy friendly, even rowdy—like a night baseball game, or sharing a heaping plate of Buffalo wings in a sports bar, or hitting a few buckets of balls at a driving range. No, there won't be an opportunity to whisper sweet nothings in each other's ears, but you may find you have an even better time and bring out the more amorous side of him if you let him engage in an activity that's super fun for him.

- If you have a crisis at work, mull over possible solutions in your mind rather than venting for forty-five minutes to friends or your guy. You may find this to be even *more* productive.

- The next time you are enjoying a great sunset, see how it feels to quietly savor it together rather than offering a running commentary.

TWENTY-FOUR

Men Really Want to Please Women

I have some really extraordinary, fabulous news to report. *Men want more than anything to please us.* I know this because every year we receive hundreds and hundreds of e-mails from guys saying that they read *Cosmo* and the main reason they offer is that they want to figure out what females need. The phrase they use most frequently is, "It's like having the other team's playbook."

Now surely in some cases they like having this playbook so they can calculate how to outsmart us—lure us into bed against our better judgment, etc. But most guys who peruse the pages simply want to know what they can do to make us happy—in bed and out of it.

Then why, you might wonder, do you occasionally feel so frustrated with the guy in your life? Why does he sometimes miss pleasing you by a landslide—like when he buys you an emergency kit for your car as a birthday gift or leaves a greasy pizza box on the coffee table all day long, with six or seven old crusts alongside it?

Here's what I've come to believe: despite how eager guys are to please us, they just don't instinctively know *how* to do it. And we refuse to tell them. We want them to just *know*—and if they don't read us or figure us out, we see it as a big fat insult.

Oh, sometimes we drop hints, and certain men take the bait.

We once had a guy admit in an interview, "God help me, I take notes. Actual freakin' notes. If she mentions what kinds of flowers she likes, I jot it down after the date. Same thing goes for music, movies, underwear, anything." But for others, the hints end up being too vague or meaningless to inspire action. What matters to women tends to be so different from what matters to men, that it's almost as if men are forced to translate another language.

So here's what you need to do: **Tell him how to please you.** Don't make him guess. Don't make him infer your desires just from knowing you. Don't set him up for a fall just to test him. Tell him:

- That your birthday is next Thursday and you're looking forward to celebrating with him.
- That you'd really like to cuddle for a few minutes right after sex.
- That there's one restaurant in particular that you'd love to go to on Saturday night.
- That when you spend the holidays with his parents, you'd love it if the two of you could sneak out one afternoon and be alone.
- That when you get home in the evening, you'd like to vent about work for ten minutes without commenting from him and when you're done to be able to ask his advice.
- That you love silver jewelry more than gold.

TWENTY-FIVE

9 Ways to Meet a Guy

Okay, admittedly it's been a while since I went man shopping (I've been married for years), but the subject still fascinates me. I'm always curious about how both readers and the young women on my staff meet guys—and the frustrations they experience along the way. Many women admit to being discouraged and annoyed because the process is "so hard." They wish it could all unfold naturally, effortlessly and romantically. After a spate of fruitless nights in bars and clubs, they feel an urge to take to their couches rather than face one more night of being "out there."

But whoever said it was supposed to be easy? I think you have to tackle meeting guys like you would any big project—by putting lots of effort into it, perfecting your skills as you go, and realizing that some strategies work a whole lot better than others. What's funny is that as soon as you accept the fact that it's a project, the whole experience feels less daunting. And you'll have far more luck.

So approach it as if you were about to buy your first apartment or plan a trip to Fiji, rather than hoping something will just happen when you show up at a party. Here are the nine best tips I've learned.

1. Don't develop hard-and-fast rules about the ways you're willing to go about your search. Some women, for in-

stance, have a policy against being fixed up. Or they refuse to ever try online dating. But you need to be flexible and willing to experiment with a variety of strategies, particularly if you find yourself in a drought. Zillions of women have met good guys on blind dates. So why turn your nose up at them? And you can't simply try one blind date and then bag the whole strategy. My theory has always been that a winning prospect only comes around every six to seven blind dates, so you may have to chitchat with five chumps in order to get there.

You also need to be flexible about the places you go to meet guys. If you head to the same bars all the time, you're going to see the same old guys—or the same type. There are always interesting *new* ways to meet men, and you need to keep your ear to the ground to hear what's hot at a given moment. It keeps changing. One minute networking cocktail parties are all the rage, and the next minute something else is. I heard lately, for instance, that day spas are starting to offer times when singles can mingle.

2. Be unashamedly proactive and methodical. Cold-hearted calculation doesn't seem like a very magical approach to meeting the love of your life, but there will be plenty of time for magic once you're dating. Tell yourself that you will do at least two specific things every week to facilitate your quest. And when opportunities present themselves, *make* things happen rather than just allowing them to unfold. For instance, if you see a hottie and there doesn't seem to be an easy way to meet him, accidentally bump into him, for God's sake.

3. If you are going to a party, bar, or event, do not travel in

huge packs of women. Women who move in wolf packs intimidate guys. It's hard to break into a group that size, plus it's easy for a guy to think that the moment he turns around after talking to you, all the other chicks are going to laugh hysterically about a comment he made or even the pants he's wearing. Two is an okay number (you and a friend) but three is even better because one friend has a pal to talk to if you start chatting someone up.

4. Avoid being *too* glam. When you're all dolled up, you may feel like a man magnet, but guys are often put off by too much product. Lots of makeup and tons of designer labels scream high maintenance, and guys say repeatedly in e-mails and interviews to us that they don't like that. Plus, all that junk makes you seem unapproachable. You want to look pretty and sexy, period. One other tip: consider wearing something that could be a conversation starter, like a T-shirt with something funny written on it or a faux-fur vest that a guy may ask to touch.

5. Have a drink in your hand. We once had a cute girl write a piece about her experience being a professional wing woman—someone hired by shy guys to chat up women in bars and then introduce them. She provided a great tip: do not stand around empty-handed. If you are holding a drink, a guy won't feel he has to immediately buy one for you. But then later, if things are going well, ordering you a refill gives him something positive to do.

6. Do not be *too* coy. Coy can be sexy and very appealing. Guys, as we know, like the chase. But if you seem *too* elusive, guys won't approach. These days, more than ever, men seem to dislike ambiguity and they shy away

from the slightest chance of rejection. So what's a coy move that works? When I was a young single writer, David Givens, anthropologist and author of *Love Signals: A Practical Guide to the Body Language of Courtship*, gave me a wonderful tip: Make eye contact with an object of desire, hold for three seconds, and then look away. Repeat. If he's interested, you've given him a pretty clear signal that it's safe to head your way. Once you're talking to a guy, you don't want to be all over him like white on rice—you'll only seem desperate. But let him know in a slightly more subtle manner that you're interested—for instance, by laying your hand on his arm when you make a point.

7. When there's an adorable guy suddenly in your path, don't be so worried about saying the perfect thing that you end up saying nothing at all. All right, you don't want to come across like an idiot, but as long as you seem fun and friendly, you'll be okay—so just get *something* out. To be better than okay, rely on a few strategies. Asking for help from a guy is a surefire conversation starter. Because you're not trying to be clever, you'll feel less self-conscious, and also, guys *love* to offer assistance. If you are in an electronics store and see an adorable guy five feet away, you can try something like "Excuse me, could you tell me the difference between LCD and plasma screen TVs?" Humor can work, too, but it's trickier. Rather than try to be the next Ellen DeGeneres, you can make a cute comment about the absurdity of a given moment. For instance, if you are standing by an elevator, you could slyly say, "I hear that

pressing the button twenty or thirty times actually *does* make it come faster."

Another good trick: playfully polling a guy. An example: "I'm taking a poll for the bar. Did you have to drive more than five miles to get here?" You could also come up with a question about yourself you toss out to him, like "Do you think I should get blue contact lenses?"

8. Be positive. A few years ago I arranged for a single friend of mine to sit next to a hot guy at a charity dinner. Through the night, I watched them from my table and I had every reason to believe things were going well. She seemed enchanted and they were both talking up a storm. But later the guy told me that my friend had offered up an endless stream of negative riffs. She hated the subway, her boss, teacup dogs, etc. She thought that confessing things she didn't like was a way of bonding with him, but guys are turned off by negativity.

9. Really hear what he has to say. When you're nervous, it's easy to become overly self-conscious. You might ask a guy you've just met plenty of questions, but be so worried about what to say next that you don't pay close attention to his answers. And that will make it harder to form a connection with him. Here's a trick to help you focus. Wait a few beats after he says something and *think* about what he's said. Then allow your next comment or question to really play off what he's told you.

TWENTY-SIX

11 Great Questions to Ask on a Date

No matter how well you click with a guy, early on in a relationship there can be clunky conversational moments when a topic has run its course and your brain suddenly freezes. You can't think of one single thing to say, and he seems momentarily tongue-tied as well. What you need is a good question, one that will not only provoke an interesting answer but will move the conversation along nicely.

Each month in *Cosmo* we offer a great question to ask a guy. They work on first dates, fifth dates, and even if you've been in a relationship for years. Though we've run many questions, I have my favorites. They easily lead to other questions and answers and they also uncover a lot about a guy. Just don't ask them all at once or he'll think you're trying to play Barbara Walters.

1. What's the best piece of advice anyone has ever given you?
2. Where do you want to visit before you die?
3. What movie do you never get tired of watching?
4. What's your favorite time of the day?
5. If you could have dinner with anyone, whom would you choose?
6. Is there anything you're superstitious about?

7. If you had an extra hour each day, how would you spend it?

8. What day of your life would you like to live over again?

9. What's the craziest dare you've ever gone through with?

10. If you had to choose, would you rather be rich or famous?

11. Do you remember who taught you to ride a bike?

TWENTY-SEVEN

The Lie Your Girlfriends Tell You About Guys

I t seems as if every decade, someone has to write a best-selling book to remind women that most guys prefer to pursue rather than be chased and that if we attempt to flip the situation, we can possibly derail a budding romance or, at the very least, waste time on a guy who could not care less.

In the nineties it was *The Rules*, the book that advised women on the essentialness of playing hard to get, of waiting for guys to ask *them* out and always being the first to end a phone call (with phrases like "Gotta go"). If women failed to play hard to get, the authors said, the men they were attracted to would soon lose interest. In this decade it was *He's Just Not That into You* by Greg Behrendt and Liz Tuccillo, which explained that when you don't hear from a man after a date, it's for one reason and one reason alone: he doesn't have any desire whatsoever to see you—despite what he might have said when he dropped you at your door or rolled out of your bed in the morning.

Why do we have to be constantly reminded that guys want to do the chasing and if they don't chase it means they're not interested? I think it's partly because our girlfriends, in an attempt to boost our spirits, frequently encourage us to take the bull by the horns. They say things like "Maybe he's been super busy" and

"Why don't you call *him*?" and "Tell him that you have tickets for a concert and you're wondering if he wants to go." Also, who wants to sit around waiting? Women have discovered how nice it is to be in control of their own destiny.

There's another reason, I think—one that's popped up in recent years. Guys have started telegraphing confusing messages. They say and do little things that make us suspect that they dig it when we make a move.

That's certainly what we've found in our *Cosmo* studies. In one, sixty-six percent of guys said they like it when women hit on them in bars. In another, seventy-eight percent said they prefer it when a woman makes the first move sexually.

So what are we supposed to believe? Are guys changing? Are *some* guys changing? Have guys secretly always wanted women to be more aggressive? How are we supposed to respond?

Here's my opinion on the matter. Guys are just as inclined as ever to want to be the pursuers. In the beginning, at least, they don't want you calling, text messaging, e-mailing, or sending cute cards with dogs on them. But they also despise rejection. Therefore, when a situation between you and a new guy reads ambiguously—and there seem to be more of those moments these days—he may look for a clear sign that you're game before he makes his move. *He wants to know that if he pursues you, you'll allow yourself to be caught.* When you "bump into" him at the bar or make the first move sexually, you're removing the ambiguity.

But *after* that, he's probably going to want to take over—if he's attracted to you, that is. As Patrick Meagher, one of the hosts of Cosmo Radio, puts it, "Open the door a little, but then let me bust through."

The bottom line is: if you really like a guy, it's best to let him do the chasing—as unfair as that may sound. You can—in the very, very beginning—give him a slight nudge if you suspect he's looking for proof of willingness on your part. But do it quickly, like a sleight of hand, and then back off. For instance, if you hit it off with him at a party, you can suggest that the two of you get together sometime. But leave it so that *he's* supposed to call you.

And what if he comes across as very responsive and *does* call you and take you out on what seems like a fun date, but then you don't hear from him? Well, he wasn't as interested as he thought. Your best girlfriend may tell you to go ahead, invite him to something, because he clearly likes you enough to ask you out. And if you do, he may even say yes to your invitation. But if a guy says yes to a second date that you initiated, there's a chance it's only out of inertia. And you're only postponing the inevitable—never hearing from him again.

TWENTY-EIGHT

Men Actually Are Men of Few Words

Of all the facts that I've learned at *Cosmo*, the one that blew me away the most is this: according to a study, the average woman speaks 6,000 to 8,000 words a day; the average man speaks 2,000 to 4,000.

I don't recall what study this statistic emerged from or whether the results have been replicated. It really doesn't matter, because like any woman who hears it, I know on a gut level that it is basically correct. If you've grown up with men, if you've worked with men, if you've *loved* men, you're aware that they just don't seem to talk as much as we do. In fact, many of them seem capable of getting by on far fewer than half the words a woman uses.

I remember the moment I really understood this in my own relationship. My husband and I had been married only a year or two, and we were on a car trip through the Adirondack Mountains. He made a comment that I considered to be totally irritating, and I told him as much. Then, miffed, I turned my attention to the scenery and didn't say another word. I wasn't going to let the experience ruin my weekend, but on the other hand, I was too annoyed to resume chatting for a while. My husband was obviously feeling the same way, because for the next hour he didn't utter a word either. Then out of the blue he pointed with his finger and announced, "Wow, look at those mountain peaks!" I could tell by the friendly, even tone of his voice that he wasn't miffed at all. If our ornery exchange an hour earlier had bugged him, he'd let it drop then and there. So for the last hour in the car, he had said nothing not because he was irritated but because *he just hadn't felt like talking.* And because I hadn't pulled him into a conversation. Up until then in our relationship I probably hadn't let an hour go by without instigating dialogue. It was my first realization that he could be perfectly happy not saying a word for long stretches of time.

Though I was given my wake-up call that day, seeing the bold statistic years later was another matter. It was stunning to behold how *big* the word gap was. There are exceptions to every rule and some women are in love with gabbers, but my guess is that you can relate personally to the 4,000-versus-8,000-word principle.

So what do we do about it? For one, take comfort in numbers and realize that it doesn't reflect inadequacy on your part that he would prefer to live with his mouth on mute a lot of the time. But that won't help the fact that you want to know your guy better and stay abreast of what's going on in his life. Here are a few ways to loosen his lips:

- **Pick your moments.** Many guys seem to be chattier at particular times of the day. Figure out what those times are. Right after work is a period when many men are too stressed to do much more than grunt, but an hour or so later, after unwinding, your honey may feel in the mood.
- **Don't pounce.** Guys shut down when you press too much or seem overly eager.
- **Catch him when he's *slightly* preoccupied.** There's been interesting research on how men feel overwhelmed if they are

forced to employ too many senses at once (poor things!). For instance, when you're sitting across the table from him, staring into his eyes and talking to him as you touch his hand it may turn into sensory overload on his end. However, if you catch him when he's absentmindedly involved in an activity or you're doing something side-by-side, he won't be forced to make intense eye contact during the conversation and he may be more responsive. Don't try this when he's watching a game or twisting a Phillips screwdriver into anything—that's not absentminded stuff. But when he's driving is a good time, or when you're taking a walk or doing dishes together after a meal.

- **Decrease the likelihood of buyer's remorse.** Let's say you're driving in the car with your guy and a little easy chatting turns into a thoughtful conversation. After you've recovered from the shock, you may feel tempted to use the opportunity with Mr. Chatty to raise a few issues that you've been concerned about—such as his recent preoccupation with Internet porn or the state of your relationship. *Stop.* Count your blessings and just keep listening. Otherwise, like a dog that's been lured into the car for a vet appointment by the aid of a liver-flavored chew toy, your guy won't allow himself to be tricked again.

If you think something's bugging him and want him to open up, see chapter 30.

TWENTY-NINE

You Really Should Take What a Guy Says Literally

A s women, we sometimes choose to load what we say with meaning that isn't totally apparent in the words we use. For instance, a friend asks how you're feeling and you respond, "Good—I guess." She knows, in part because she's a girl, too, not to be misled by the word *good*. The correct translation? "I'm not so good but I need you to keep probing because it's hard for me to spit it out." (Or perhaps, "I'm not so good but I need you to keep probing because you're part of the problem.")

Because *we* do this, we assume men do it, too, and when we have the slightest feeling that a man is being less than direct, we push him to cough up what he *really* thinks or feels.

I've known from the research I've seen that guys are very literal when they speak. But I don't think I was totally convinced until I read the mail at *Cosmo* and saw how baffled guys are by women's failure to take them literally and by our unrelenting desire to read things into both their words and their tone of voice. One guy asked in an interview, "Why do women always assume something is *wrong*? I was on the phone with this girl, and I guess my tone was a little off. She kept asking 'Are you okay? Why did you say that?'"

Oh sure, on occasion some guys are cagey as hell—or totally

duplicitous. And sometimes a guy who's in a funk will sulk and force you to use a crowbar to uncover why he's acting crabby toward you all of a sudden. But for the most part, guys mean what they say. And because of that, you generally should take what a guy says at face value and not go crazy trying to analyze it—or probing for more info.

When he tells you he's fine, for example, chances are he is (unless there's real evidence to the contrary). When you ask him if he wants Italian or Mexican and he answers "Mexican," he really, really wants Mexican. He's not just saying that to be polite, or in the hopes you'll dig deeper for the truth.

So don't ask, "Are you sure?" "Really?" or "You're not just saying that, are you?" It drives a guy nuts.

THIRTY

2 Secrets to Getting Him to Open Up

Sometimes it's not just *talking* you're looking for from a guy. Sometimes what you want is for him to *spill*—to divulge what he's really thinking about and, if you're lucky, what he's really feeling. Maybe he's seemed like a sad puppy every time he's walked in the door lately, and you sense there's a problem at work but he hasn't fessed up yet. Or maybe you're worried that something's bugging him about *you*. Or maybe you've just met him and wish you knew him better.

Of all the advice I've read on this subject, there's one strategy that's always stayed with me, perhaps because it's not only good but also so simple to remember. It's from New-York-based psychologist Alon Gratch, author of *If Men Could Talk: Translating the Secret Language of Men*, who says that if you want a guy to come clean, you need to do two simple things: be both *casual* and *concrete*.

Casual, he told me, because men feel inherently vulnerable when they open up. To them, revealing is equivalent to being weak. Also, he says, men fear losing their autonomy and independence, a by-product of their need to escape their early dependence on their mothers. When they sense that you're plumbing the depths for info that will help you possess them, they become evasive or silent. "To help them open up," Dr. Gratch says, "don't make a big deal of the issue, just present your ques-

101

tion casually." For instance, rather than gravely ask "What's wrong? You seem really upset," keep your remark easy, like "Work must be crazy right now, huh?" You might also try the side-by-side technique I mentioned in the last chapter—talk in the car, for example. Or even on the phone. This will help keep matters on the casual side.

Now for the *concrete* part. We females tend to be more nuanced in conversation and we often ask questions in a vague or roundabout way so we don't come across as too blunt. We also value emotional gradations in verbal exchanges. But men, says Gratch, believe that the purpose of communication is to exchange information, and they respond best to very clear and straightforward statements. "Plus, they're action oriented," he says. "They want to fix, not dwell on the problem." So if you want to help a man open up, use concrete-action–oriented words. Instead of asking "How do you feel about your meeting with your boss tomorrow?" try "What's your strategy for the meeting with your boss tomorrow?"

The same approach works when you're talking about your relationship. Announcing "I don't feel like I know you these days" will seem *insane* to him. Instead try "Maybe we can talk about something other than work tonight."

THIRTY-ONE

9 Topics That Make Guys Gag

In addition to the other points I've made about getting a guy to open up, avoiding the following topics will make him much more receptive to talking.

1. **Celebrity gossip.** Most guys don't give a damn about Jen, Brad, Angelina, Reese, Britney, Leo, Tom, Kate, Jessica, or anyone else in Hollywood, no matter how big of a scandal has just erupted in their lives or how heartbroken or bulimic they may be. In fact, a man is likely to be suspicious of why *you* care so much—and why you consider yourself on a first-name basis with people you've never met.

2. **Shoes.** This includes any talk about cute shoes, shoes you gotta have, shoes that cost half your paycheck, shoes you didn't buy but should have, shoes you bought but *shouldn't* have, shoes that kill your feet, and shoes other women are wearing.

3. **Catty gossip about your friends.** It makes them seriously question what kind of person you are.

4. **Anything involving below-the-belt functions or problems.** That would include bloating, cramps, menstrual flow, yeast infections, discharge, itchiness, soreness, and yes, gas. One of the things I've laughed at most at *Cosmo*

was this comment from a guy for a story we were doing about conversation between the sexes: "For some reason," he wrote, "an old girlfriend felt compelled to tell me that she gets rid of gas pains by laying on her side, bringing her leg to her chest, and then 'letting it seep out.' Any guy who's okay with hearing that should be shot."

5. **Your weight, your "fatness," or your dieting plans.**

6. **Old boyfriends.** Including just casual references—like a rock-climbing excursion you went on together or what kind of car he owned.

7. **People you know only peripherally.** Like the girl in your department at work who's already called in sick seven days this year or the guy at the gym who purses his lips in this really bizarre way when he runs on the treadmill.

8. **The state of your union.** There will be times when you have to put a relationship issue onto the table. Do not announce, "We have to talk about our relationship." Guys absolutely hate to talk about the relationship. (See chapter 30, "2 Secrets to Getting Him to Open Up.")

9. **What the two of you are experiencing *right now.*** Women love to capture the moment with words. We'll make remarks like "I'm so happy right now, aren't you?" or "Isn't this music great?" Guys prefer to *experience* the moment— without having to hear a play-by-play of it.

THIRTY-TWO

How to Get Your Guy to Listen More

E arlier I described tricks for helping a man to open up. When you read the suggestions, though, you may have been wondering, *What about me, for God's sake?* You may feel that you do all this work to encourage him to release his innermost thoughts and desires, but when it's your turn to spill, your guy can't get any traction on your words. Oh, he may sit there dutifully on the couch, but in the midst of your soul baring you notice that he starts appearing distracted or pained or weirded out and maybe he even starts channel-surfing (since when you sat down and said you wanted to talk, all he did was put the TV on mute). At moments like this, you really have to fight the urge not to throw a large heavy object at his head.

Well, your guy may never become the listener you imagine in your fantasies, but you can help him be much better at the job.

Remember what I suggested about undertaking side-by-side activities when you want a guy to be talky? This strategy also works well when you need him to listen. You're likely to find that he actually pays more attention while you're jogging together or walking along the beach or driving in the car and he doesn't have to deal with as much sensory stimulation. Since guys like rituals and routine, you can also use this to your advantage. You can set up a regular activity—perhaps a Sunday morning pancake feast—that allows for easy conversation and that will eventually evolve into a time when you always catch up. Just don't jinx it by telling friends in front of him that Sunday is when you always do your "chatathon."

Okay, you've got time and location down, but you may still have to help him along. Michael Gurian, a social philosopher, therapist, and author of *What Could He Be Thinking?* told me that one of the best ways to engage men as listeners is to first learn to edit yourself. (Brutal to hear but in my case, at least, so true.) "The key thing a woman can do is cut down on the number of words she uses—in other words, plan out a little bit better how she is going to get to her point." Men are good listeners, he says, when people cut to the chase. "They are bad listeners when people are very tangential and link gobs of sensory and emotional details together."

What if you're a gabber by nature and you enjoy long conversations? Well, it may be time to tell yourself that though your guy does many things for you, this isn't going to be one of them. Save lengthy ruminations, stream of consciousness, and play-by-play work sagas for your gal pals and any male friends who seem to find it enjoyable for some reason. With your partner, trim, trim, trim away the extraneous.

Of course, you don't just want him to listen, you want him to ask questions, too. As a friend of mine once said, there's nothing more intoxicating than dating a guy who knows how to do "Q and A." Gurian says that a guy will ask more questions when he is clear on what the topic of conversation is—as well as what you want from him. If you just offer up a myriad of feelings/thoughts/memories/connections, he may not be able to keep up with it very well. "In his mind, there's no topic, there are just feelings," says Gurian. Say something like "My boss chewed me out today.

I need to tell you what happened and then get your advice on how I should handle things tomorrow," or "My sister has been acting kind of odd toward me lately. Can I describe her behavior to you and get your take on whether you think something is the matter?"

Since he knows what his role in the conversation is, he's likely to ask questions that enable him to be better in that role and give you whatever help and advice you need. Like "It sounds like your boss is just in a bad mood. I wouldn't worry unless it happens again."

Granted, sometimes you don't want his advice. You just want to talk so you experience catharsis. This is hard for many guys to relate to, but again, just tell him what you expect. You could say something like "All I want to do is vent and then have you hold me."

I know it seems to be a lot of heavy lifting on your part, but if you slip into a groove with it—picking your moments, letting him know where you're headed—it won't seem so forced and calculated over time.

I bet I know a thought that flashed through your mind while you were reading this: *Why did he seem to be such a good listener when we were first dating?* Gurian has the explanation. "Men ask more questions, and in fact listen better, when they are courting, in the throes of flirtatious love, and anticipating sex."

It's something for you to consider even now in your relationship, says Gurian. More flirting and more sex often lead to more listening.

THIRTY-THREE

Guys Just Don't Notice Things

A couple of years ago a forty-something friend of mine, a divorced mother of two teens, told me a hilarious story about a new guy she was dating. The guy was a warm and generous man and loved doing things for her. One day, as a surprise, he gave her a big Coach tote bag—because as a mom and a TV producer, she lugged a ton of stuff around. She happens to be more of a Marc Jacobs bag kind of chick, but she was so touched by his thoughtfulness that she immediately abandoned her other bags and began carrying this one around. And it did have many nice features. For instance, there was a little pouch on the end of the bag for a water bottle. One small mystery was the padded square of material inside the bag, but when she asked her beau what its purpose was, he thought for a second and said the pad was to wrap her laptop in so it didn't knock around. *Wow,* she thought. *This bag has everything.*

Six months later, still besotted with her beau and still lugging the bag around, she walked into a fancy cocktail party with it. A woman she didn't know glanced at the bag and smiled. "Oh, you've got the Coach diaper bag, too," she remarked to her. "It's great, isn't it?"

My friend's jaw dropped. For six months she had been carrying around a freakin' diaper bag. And, of course, it now all made sense. The pouch was for a baby bottle. The pad was for changing a diaper while on the run. She cringed as she reflected on all the high-powered meetings she'd been to with the bag in tow. Her boyfriend had told her it was a tote, so she'd just believed him.

And since he was the one who'd purchased it, why hadn't he known it was a diaper bag, for chrissakes? Because he's a guy. He'd noticed this big bag in a store and thought, *My girlfriend needs a big bag.* And he hadn't paid attention to the details screaming *baby.*

The funny thing is that around the same time as my friend told me this story, a reader wrote in to say that her boyfriend had bought her a kind of ugly shirt for a gift and when she tried it on, she realized that it was a maternity top.

Guys are visual creatures, true, but they don't always notice the details.

According to psychologist Dr. Jay Carter, men actually have fewer rods in their eyes than women, which means they aren't always seeing what *we're* seeing.

You can't help him see better, but to avoid frustration, give him detailed directions when you're asking him to do things for you.

- If, let's say, you want him to pick up mustard for the chicken with tarragon-mustard sauce that you're preparing for dinner tonight, tell him specifically what kind you want or you will end up not with the gourmet mustard that you *always* have in your fridge and that he must have seen a million times, but the bright yellow kind that's meant for hot dogs.
- If you know he's considering earrings as a gift for you, tell him whether your ears are pierced or not, because he may have no idea whatsoever.

- If you want him to help you clean up after a party, do not say, "Can you straighten up the living room?" Because his idea of clean is not likely to be the same as yours. Instead say, "I'd love your help cleaning up. Will you please pick up the beer cans, vacuum the tortilla chips up from the rug, and wipe that large blob of dip off the floor?"

THIRTY-FOUR

In Love, Consider Yourself an Agent Provocateur

One of the lessons I learned about love long before I landed at *Cosmo* was that women are generally the ones who make sure a relationship is humming. I don't mean they alone keep it alive emotionally, but rather that they put themselves in charge of quality control, and if they detect trouble, they will do their best to correct it.

For instance, it's so often the woman who plans the fun and sexy activities—whether it's a week under mosquito netting at a tropical resort or a midnight picnic in August to watch the Perseid meteor shower. In *Cosmo*, in fact, we rarely let a year go by without mentioning the freaking Perseid meteor shower and why you should grab your guy, a blanket, and a bottle of wine and make out under the endless shooting stars.

I guess I grew up knowing that this kind of stuff fell more to women, but it was first articulated to me by a marriage counselor whom I worked with at another magazine. "Women are the *caretakers* of relationships," she told me. She explained that it comes fairly naturally to us, programmed, perhaps, because of our prehistoric job as keepers of the hearth. But we also do it to fill the void because men tend *not* to take on this assignment—at least they don't after those early giddy days. Okay, you may be in the fifth year of a relationship with a guy who regularly throws open the door and says things like "Pack a bag, baby—I've got us booked for the weekend in this great B and B in the Berkshires," and if you are, fantastic. But your guy is far more the exception than the rule.

Though the caretaker part may come naturally to women, over time in a relationship it's easy to grow a little tired of it, even, dare I say, downright sick of it—especially all the activity planning and especially if you are the only one doing the heavy lifting. And as a result of your boredom, you may begin to slack off. And once you do, your relationship could suffer the consequences. Guys may not feel an inclination to plan activities like picnics under the stars, but they enjoy them and love thrives when there's fun and unexpected activities going on.

This leaves you between a rock and a hard place. If you do too much caretaking, you resent it; if you let go of the responsibility, your relationship can grow stale. But I think there are two strategies that can make the caretaking role easier for you:

- First, turn around the way you look at the role. Instead of seeing it as tedious, something that you do more than your fair share of, try viewing it as this specialty you have as a woman, something you do because you're brilliant at it.

    A few years ago I was editing an article that touched on the subject and I commented to my longtime assistant Miriam about the disparity between men and women. She then said something that flipped everything around for me.

    "It's so boring to think of yourself as a caretaker," she said. "Maybe it's better for a woman to think of herself as an *agent provocateur*." I loved that concept. Of course, she didn't mean it literally. An agent provocateur is someone who goes undercover and incites people to riot. But if you use the term loosely, to describe someone who is secretive and naughty, someone who likes to make mischief and cause unexpected things to happen, there's a very sexy feeling to it.

- You can also inspire a man to take more initiative in keeping the relationship exciting—but you're going to have to tell him exactly what you're looking for. Women dislike doing this because they think it's more romantic if the guy comes up with all this stuff on his own. Let go of that idea and in the long run you'll get more of what you want from him.

Tell your guy that you would love to have him plan Friday night. Start with a compliment—"You always have fun ideas"—and suggest that he pick out the movie or where you go for dinner. You can't complain, however, when he takes you to the kind of restaurant where there are dartboards and pool tables. Eventually you can even suggest he devise the whole evening. The more practice he gets and the more confident he feels, the more likely he is to surprise you with plans before you've even asked.

THIRTY-FIVE

What You Must Burn Immediately

One of the pleasures of moving into a steady relationship with a guy is that you can finally let your guard down about your appearance and not worry about looking model-perfect a hundred percent of the time. If one night you feel like slipping into a comfy pair of flannel pajamas, you just do it. You know he's not going to be horrified. In fact, he may even compliment you on how cute you look in your little jammies.

Over time you become less rigid about other matters, too. You skip makeup when you feel like it, don't shave your legs *every* day, wear sweats around the house at night even if he's at your place, and on days when, as one of my editors once said, your butt needs a hug, you go so far as to pull on a pair of granny panties. It's terrific to feel secure enough about yourself and your relationship that you don't always have to be glammed up. Over time you may even find yourself in sweats more often than not.

Here's the problem, though: guys just don't like it when you fall too far into a comfort zone about your appearance. They want you to look nice, dress nice, smell nice, and feel nice, too (soft skin, no prickly leg hair) *much* of the time. When you continually let things slide, he notices—and minds. You may be thinking how wonderful it is not to be a freakin' slave to your looks around him, but he's bummed. As a guy once mournfully asked when we interviewed him for a relationship article: "Who kidnapped my sex kitten?"

One factor at the root of this issue is that men are visual creatures and become aroused by visual stimuli. As psychologist Stan Katz says, "The way you look and dress will always be a driving force in a man's attraction to you." Think about when the two of you met. You probably couldn't miss the fact that his eyes were glued to your legs or your boobs or your face or all of the above. On your early dates, he probably said things like "You smell so good," or "You have great hair," or "I love that dress." Not exactly Wordsworth, but intoxicating nonetheless. And you loved the fact that he was riveted by your appearance and told you so.

Remove that fabulous visual stimulation, however, and you're taking away something that he craves and that fuels his arousal. Also, he may be bummed that you don't seem to be going to any effort anymore. So why did he mislead you by telling you that he loved you in those flannel jammies or that he thought your hair looked so cute in a ponytail? Maybe because the novelty intrigued him initially—it added an element of surprise to the visual stimulation. And why doesn't he speak up when he starts to have a problem? Because guys are famous for leaving well enough alone. He may drop a few hints, but otherwise he'll avoid rocking the boat. He may not even consciously realize how much your new low-maintenance routine is bugging him.

None of this means that you have to be all obsessive again, wearing lip gloss to bed and going through a pack of razor blades every week. But ask yourself if you've crossed a line from being relaxed with him to being out-and-out lazy. Have you deep-sixed the very things he found so beguiling about you? Some questions worth answering: When was the last time you . . .

- Rubbed lotion all over your body before you climbed into bed?
- Wore an item of clothing that you recall made him practically eat his heart out?
- Applied fragrance when you arrived home from work or dressed up on Saturday?
- Bought something very flimsy at Victoria's Secret—and wore it?
- Had a pedicure?
- Went to bed in an item of clothing that was not made of jersey, terry cloth, or flannel?
- Went to bed totally naked?
- Got a bikini wax?
- Looked good in a way that could best be characterized as "smokin'"?

If the answer to most of these is weeks ago (or longer!), it's time to make an effort again and get back into some of your old grooming and dressing routines. Reflect on his early compliments and let those be your inspiration. For instance, if he always raved about your hair, unshackle it from the scrunchy and blow-style the hell out of it. And though you can save a pair or two of granny panties for gloomy days, burn the rest!

Lastly, don't overlook the power of visual surprise. A colleague told me a fun story about charging up her husband that way. She felt that things were a little blah between them, so one night when they were going out to dinner, she sat at the makeup table in her bedroom with no top on, just this amazing push-up bra. Her husband kept walking back and forth, in and out of the room, and she could tell he was turned on by the sight of her. Finally he walked over to her and started fondling her, and then suggested they have a romp in the sack before they went to dinner. Afterward, as they were dressing, he commented on the fact that she was putting on a different bra.

"I thought you were wearing that push-up bra tonight," he said.

She said she loved smiling coyly at him and announcing, "No, I was never planning on wearing that out tonight."

THIRTY-SIX

Why You *Shouldn't* Be
Soul Mates with Him

The idea of being someone's soul mate sounds really, really good. The dictionary defines *soul mate* simply as someone temporarily suited to another, but in popular culture it's come to mean so much more. Your soul mate *gets* you completely, knows what makes you tick and what you long for. He senses what's on your mind before you do, loves sharing *everything* with you, and supports all that you do. Gosh, I'm getting all misty-eyed just thinking about it.

It should come as no surprise when I tell you that most women find the soul mate concept appealing. According to research by the Intelligence Group, the trend-tracking company I've worked with for years, almost ninety percent of women say they want to marry a guy who fulfills that role for them. How could you blame them? And yet here's the problem. Being soul mates with your guy or trying to turn your guy into one may not be such a sensational idea.

First of all, being a woman's soul mate is an awfully tall order to fill, and many good guys can't come within chick-approved distance of delivering perfectly on that front. And that can lead to all sorts of misery. You become frustrated, for instance, when he doesn't listen to your stories with bug-eyed enthusiasm or want to gaze in awe at twinkly Christmas lights the way you do.

Also, and perhaps more important, it's possible that being each other's soul mate is at odds with being one smoking hot couple. A year ago I went to a conference where I had a chance to meet Dr. Lana Holstein, who is managing director of medical programs at the Miraval Resort and the author with her husband of *Your Long Erotic Weekend*. She told me that one of the concerns she hears most from couples she counsels in workshops is that the spark is gone from the relationship. The culprit, she says, is often the fact that the two partners are working real hard at being soul mates.

"These days we want our partner to be our lover, supporter, confidant, and bestest, bestest friend," explains Dr. Holstein. "But when you become so alike and share so much, you're in danger of losing the masculine and feminine energy. Rather than being like two opposite ends of a magnet, you're both like the center. And then you lose the juiciness of attraction."

But you have *needs*, you may be saying. Who will help you sort out your work problems? Who will go to the Christmas tree lighting with you? Who will share that jumbo bag of sour-cream-and-chive chips with you when you're PMSing? Hey, there's a reason they invented girlfriends and *Cosmopolitan*s. It's so you can share certain information and activities with *them*. It's also great to go it alone on occasion. Remove from your guy the burden of being everything to you. See what happens if you:

- Stop telling him every single detail about your day.
- Discuss certain life concerns just with your girlfriend and not him.

- Have rituals that you do all by yourself.
- Have at least one hobby that you do all on your own.
- Don't feel you have to fight to the finish and work through every problem before going to bed. (Many experts today feel that it's good to accept that you won't resolve everything.)
- Get back into the habit of having a girl's night out once a week or so.
- Go away sometimes for a weekend on your own.
- Pee with the door closed.

Chances are you'll find that the glorious "juiciness" returns when there's a little mystery and more to learn about each other.

THIRTY-SEVEN

How to Tell When a Man Has Something Important to Tell You

Because body language plays such an important part in how we communicate, not only in a love relationship but also in other areas of our lives, I've read an enormous amount on the subject in the past few years. It's been fascinating to discover the messages we send with our eyes and mouths and hands and shoulders. Knowing what certain nonverbal cues mean can be very useful. It can help you translate in tricky situations.

One of my favorite body language tidbits: when a man purses his lips or puckers his mouth, it often means he has something on his mind that he wants to tell you, but hasn't quite formulated the words yet.

Your best strategy is to stay where you are, keep the mood light, and don't launch into a whole new topic. Whatever you do, resist the urge to yank out the forceps and ask, "What's the matter?" Anthropologist and body language expert David Givens says that pursed lips suggest that your guy *wants* to share. You just have to allow him time (and the right atmosphere) to spit it out.

However, if he pauses in the middle of speaking and the tip of his tongue pokes out like a little lizard head, then there's information he's nervous about revealing—and he's trying to *prevent* it from jumping out. The info might not be negative—perhaps it's just a situation at work that he would love to unload but feels embarrassed about.

If the information is not really negative, you may be able to ease it out of him. Chances are it relates to what you were just talking about. So Givens suggests circling back to that topic in a little while. That may encourage him to spill.

THIRTY-EIGHT

11 Fascinating Facts About Cheating

I was originally going to write a chapter on how to tell if a guy is cheating. Then I thought no, maybe I should do something on how to *prevent* a guy from cheating. Then I thought maybe I should do a chapter on what it means if *you're* the one who's cheating—since today, according to experts, women appear to be cheating almost as much as men. Then I decided that it might be better to pull together everything I've learned about the whole subject of infidelity.

It's easy to find yourself slightly obsessed about cheating these days, considering that it appears to be rampant, and even couples that seem brilliantly happy are being rocked by it. How's this for irony? Recently I was going through back issues of *Cosmo* and I found an article we ran in 2003 on cheat-proofing your relationship. This was the first line of the piece: "You and your man could have a love that's tighter than Jen and Brad's and still not be immune to infidelity." God, we were dead right: No one is completely immune. You can hire a nanny who looks like a Hummer and make sure your guy never shoots a movie with Angelina Jolie, but that doesn't ensure that he won't stray—or you won't either for that matter. But understanding why both men and women cheat and learning a few tips on safeguarding your relationship gives you the best protection possible. Here's what I've come to know about cheating:

1. For men, cheating is sometimes simply a crime of opportunity. A hot chick comes on to him when he's out of town and he can't resist. One of my staffers was having dinner with her boyfriend recently, and I told her that if she picked his brain and brought back ten guy truths, I'd take care of the tab. She gladly accepted my offer. The number one item on his list of truths: "All guys want to cheat. The reason some choose not to is because they're afraid of getting caught."

2. Though sometimes a guy succumbs to the risk because he finds himself turned on by a new woman one night (and considers the odds of getting caught to be low), it's not that simple in most cases. From what I've learned in the past few years, guys generally cheat because there is something missing in the relationship, some hole that you may not even be conscious of. Maybe there's a lack of excitement or you're not paying as much attention to him as you used to (a familiar complaint when there's a new baby in the picture) or—a common culprit—there's not enough sex. A woman can convince herself that a falloff in sex is fine with her guy because it's fine with *her*, but most guys aren't happy with it.

   Women, by the way, do cheat as a result of pure lust or a yearning for excitement, but it's more often a result of what's going on in the relationship. A woman may feel underappreciated or believe that her guy has not lived up to her expectations—he doesn't make enough money or help out enough, for instance.

3. Hollywood types always seem to cheat with their co-stars, which makes you think movie sets are a real hot-bed, but

actually *any kind of work setting can be a danger zone.*
According to one therapist, over sixty percent of the un-
faithful men she counsels have cheated with a woman
they met at work.

Sometimes it starts innocently. Two co-workers become
friendly, swap superficial details about each other's lives,
start having lunch. But over time the details they share become more personal and the sexual energy intensifies.
Lunch leads to drinks. Perhaps the guy divulges frustrations about his love relationship and his co-worker listens
sympathetically. She begins to act more caring than his
partner—and suddenly he's committing what's sometimes
referred to as emotional adultery. He's on a slippery
slope and from there it's easy to take the friendship to the
next level: a physical one.

Women can fall into the same trap—with either a co-
worker or a male friend. You gab, you share, you flirt a
little, perhaps with no initial intention of crossing any
lines. But then you hit a speed bump in your romantic relationship and, annoyed or frustrated, you allow yourself
to slip into *dirty* flirting, and things progress from there.

4. This is a wonderful piece of wisdom I learned from a marriage expert who advocates proactivity over letting fate
take its course. Rather than simply sitting back and wor-
rying that it might happen, you *can* actually take steps to
prevent your guy from having his head turned. Do not
give your guy a reason to look elsewhere. Pay attention
to any signals that he wants sex more often and/or he's
frustrated with aspects of your relationship. If you feel
you're in a rut, see chapter 36, "Why You *Shouldn't* Be

Soul Mates with Him," and chapter 65, "How to Keep Your Sex Life Red Hot." Think of it as preventive maintenance.

Also, don't hesitate to drop by your guy's workplace occasionally. Granted, this does bear a resemblance to a black Labrador marking its territory, but it sends a clear "He's mine, bitch, things are good, and don't you dare go there" signal to any predators. Also, you put a face to your name and that may cause a co-worker to feel too guilty to pursue your man. Be honest. How long has it been since you picked up your guy at work so that the two of you could grab lunch together?

5. If you feel your guy is spending too much time with a female co-worker or gal pal, don't chew him out. That will only give him something to complain about to this person. Instead, sit down with him and calmly explain that you're uncomfortable with the amount of time he's with this woman after hours or how much he talks to her on the phone. Tell him you want him to change that. Hopefully this will be the wake-up call he needs.

6. There really *are* common warning signs of cheating. There's likely to be a significant drop in how much he wants to hang out with you; he'll be distracted or bored with you; his sexual interest in you plummets; he'll start biting your head off without provocation (the stress cheater's feelings often morph into irrational anger directed at the cheated-on one). If you suspect he's cheating, there's a decent chance he is—unless you're hopelessly paranoid. As I explain in chapter 20, "3 Se-

crets to Getting a Golden Gut," when you feel something, there's a reason.

7. Before you confront him, try to obtain proof. Guys know that if you accuse them on a hunch and they just keep denying it, you may eventually accept their explanation because you *want* to. But if you have evidence, you can't be bullshitted. When you do talk to him, fight the urge to smash his face in. Staying calm and quiet will encourage him to be more forthcoming. If you want to save the relationship, you need to learn what he views as the problem and how serious the *other* relationship is. Even if you want to kick his sorry ass to the curb, it doesn't hurt to hear him out. The more info you garner now, the less you'll be tortured by unanswered questions later.

8. If he says he's sorry and wants the two of you to work it out, you'll have to determine his commitment to that concept, as well as your own. What is your gut telling you? Can you forgive him? Do you sense you can repair the damage? Is he likely to do it again? Experts say that though some men really are cheataholics, a guy won't necessarily cheat again if you address the reason for his infidelity. If you do try to stay together, you have to be willing to stop dwelling on his infraction. You can't hold it over him, even when you're pissed as hell.

9. And what about you? If you are in a relationship but find yourself in heavy flirt mode with another guy, ask yourself why? Sure, he may be hot, but is something missing in your own relationship? If you don't want to jeopardize your relationship, don't put yourself in situations with your flirt object that have the potential to be sexually charged.

So if it's a work buddy, say no to lunch and drinks and avoid unnecessary contact. If it's a male friend, call a moratorium on your get-togethers until things cool down. Don't tell yourself, *Hey, nothing's happened* yet. If there's chemistry, it will only build if you stay in contact.

10. If you do cheat, think about what motivated you. If you feel you really want to stay in the existing relationship, address what problems between the two of you made you yearn for someone else. And don't, I repeat *don't*, confess. You may feel an urge to come clean and clear your conscience, but experts generally advise against this kind of purge because it may cause irreparable damage. Instead commit to not cheating again.

11. And what if you meet a guy who has cheated in a previous relationship? Listen to his story closely. If he strayed only when the relationship was on the rocks, it's less likely to mean he's prone to infidelity.

THIRTY-NINE

5 Signs a Guy Is Lying

Sometimes we just know when a guy is bullshitting us. He's feeling so sheepish it shows on his face, or else you've heard enough variations on his line to know it lacks any authenticity (such as when he says "I didn't even notice her").

On other occasions, though, it's not nearly as apparent. Perhaps he's had time to sturdy himself, to practice looking sincere or indignant. You may sense something's wrong but not know what. I'm happy to report that, according to body language experts, there are subtle indications that a man (or a woman, too, for that matter) is fibbing.

1. He folds his arms across his chest or crosses his legs or ankles. This is a protective move triggered by any discomfort he feels. Also, he's subconsciously closing himself off. It's as if he's telling you, "Don't trust a word I'm saying."

2. He rubs the outside corner of his eye with his finger. Even a good liar can have a hard time looking you in the eye when he's saying an untruth. By fiddling with his eye or the skin around it, he's doing his best to break eye contact.

3. He tugs at his ear. Subconsciously the liar uses hand gestures as a distraction. You're forced to notice what he's doing with his hand rather than focus on his words.

4. He rubs his finger up and down the side of his nose. It's

thought that nose rubbing is an unconscious effort to block the untruthful message emanating from the mouth. Another theory: when a person lies, he's uncomfortable and his pulse is pounding. Blood rushes to the face, causing both the nose and the ears to feel itchy. This can result in an urge to scratch them.

5. He bites his lower lip. Another subconscious protective device. It's as if he's fighting the urge to totally fess up.

FORTY

Guys Don't Give Clear Warning Before They Leave

This scary little piece of info surfaces from time to time when we are talking to experts about the dynamics in relationships and the communication issues couples face, and no matter how many times I hear it, it never fails to make me anxious.

Women don't like to imagine that a relationship could just end out of the blue, without any real warning, but it *does* happen. You could be sitting across from each other at a restaurant and have him suddenly announce that it's not working for him anymore. Or maybe he tries to be more diplomatic and says he thinks you could both use some time apart. It's hard for women to picture this occurring because if we have an issue, we put it smack on the table. We practically beg the guy to talk about it.

But lots of men are uncomfortable putting things on the table. One of the activities guys dread most is the "relationship talk," and so they'll avoid it at all costs. A guy may be troubled by aspects of the relationship, but he'll let them build until one day he's just had enough and then drops the bomb. And at this advanced stage of his discontent, it may be hard to turn the tide.

That's why you need to actively keep your finger on the pulse of your relationship. (It may seem unfair that this is yet one other thing you're in charge of, but think of it as compensating for different communication styles.)

How do you know whether you've got a problem on your hands? Chances are if he's discontent, he won't seem exactly like himself. He may also be less communicative, less willing to connect emotionally with you, and even less willing to have sex. You may have ascribed his behavior to another cause—like stress— but it's time to ask yourself if it's related to your relationship.

Raise the topic without drama and get straight to the point. Example: "You seem a little preoccupied lately. Is there something bothering you that you'd like to talk about with me?" Don't rush to fill the silence if he doesn't immediately spit it out. Give him time. If he insists that it's just work or his parents or something not involving you at all, don't press him, but keep a watch on the situation. If weeks go by and things still don't seem right—particularly the sex—then you need to take the bull by the horns. Tell him you know something is the matter, that it's distressing you, and that he needs to tell you where things stand between you.

FORTY-ONE

How to Hook a Man Forever

O f all the experts I've met in my job, one of the most fascinating is Dr. Helen Fisher, the professor of anthropology at Rutgers University whom I mentioned earlier. She's also an expert on love and the author of *Why We Love: The Nature and Chemistry of Romantic Love.* Dr. Fisher has studied love every which way, including by doing MRI scans on the brains of people who were hopelessly infatuated.

Every six weeks or so I like to have people we feature in the magazine stop by and give a "salon" talk to the staff, and I was so pleased that Dr. Fisher agreed to do this. Her presentation had my staff riveted. Let's face it: their interest in her findings wasn't purely business. They were hoping to learn things that they could put to good use in their personal lives.

One of Dr. Fisher's theories, and she mentions this in her book *Why We Love,* is that the wild, lustful rush we experience when we first fall in love is unfortunately short-lived—it generally lasts from eighteen months to three years. If the relationship survives past this point, you move into a more comfy phase and your infatuation transforms into warm, fuzzy feelings. Most of us know this from experience and accept it about love. In some cases it's even a relief not to feel insane, disoriented, and obsessed 24/7. But moving out of the infatuation phase can be treacherous. You may truly miss the pulse pounding and begin to lose interest in your partner when he no longer triggers it. The same thing could happen to your guy.

But during her lecture to us, Dr. Fisher dropped a wonderful bombshell. She said it's possible to trick the brain into feeling wildly in love, and thus keep that rush alive in your relationship. We waited with bated breath for her to explain *how*. She said that the secret is to constantly do *novel, unexpected* things as a couple. "Participating in novel experiences releases dopamine," she told us. "That in turn triggers lust and desire." Dopamine is the same chemical flooding your brain when you become infatuated with someone.

The more I thought about it, the more I could see the truth in what she said. Just think about some of the experiences you've had in the past. Maybe one day you were out for a drive with your guy and you decided to head down a road just to see where it took you. You ended up eating in a charming out-of-the-way restaurant along the side of a canal, and the next thing you knew, you were looking at your guy feeling totally giddy.

Not every novel experience works. Sometimes they backfire, like when you head out on a road trip and the car's fan belt snaps, or the supposedly cute bed-and-breakfast ends up resembling the Bates Motel, but the more you experiment, the more chances you will have to experience the rush. Surprise your guy with a night trip to an amusement park (bumper cars required); go white-water rafting; play pool in a dive bar; use a Sunday to drop in at open houses of luxury homes for sale; arrange to have massages together in one of those new "couple rooms" that day spas offer. And most fun of all, take turns arranging mystery dates for each other, assigning one night of the weekend to him and the other to you.

FORTY-TWO

How Not to End Up in an Endless String of Bad Relationships

In the past eight years I've been privy to tons of good relationship advice, lots of which I've even incorporated into my personal life. Sometimes I hear a piece of wisdom that's even *more* than good; it will strike me as bold and fresh or maybe it's simply a blunt new way of stating a fact most of us know on a certain level but haven't fully acknowledged.

The advice I'm about to share is exactly that kind. It comes from Judith Sherven, Ph.D., co-author of *Be Loved for Who You Really Are*, and it's for any woman who has had a string of relationships that just didn't work out. If you're one of those women, your first instinct may be to rail or whine to the universe, asking why there are so many sucky men out there or why your luck is so disastrous. Sometimes there doesn't seem to be much you can *do* about it.

Get ready because Sherven's advice may make you wince when you read it. Here goes: "Recognize that whenever there's a series of failed relationships, the only thing that is consistent is *you*, so you're the one who ought to make a few changes."

Stings a bit, doesn't it? But it also puts all the control in your hands for remedying the matter. You need to figure out what *you* are doing wrong. Why are you drawn to guys who, in the end, aren't a good fit for you? Do you sabotage relationships once you're in them? Do you work hard enough to sort out issues or just bolt? Friends can be of assistance if you really dare to listen to them, hear what they have to say without becoming defensive, and not hold the truth against them. Therapy can also help you understand why you pick out the same kind of guy each time. The first step is to recognize that *you're* the common denominator.

PART FOUR

YOU ON TOP

Sex

FORTY-THREE

Think with Your Panties

Chances are you know from personal experience that in general men have sex on the brain more than women do. Studies totally bear this out. One national poll found that seventy percent of men think of sex every day, compared to only thirty-four percent of women. And forty-three percent of men think about sex several times a day, while just thirteen percent of women do. And that's across the *general* population. From all the research I've seen on younger guys it seems as if they are almost never *not* thinking about getting it on. If you had a daily printout from the brain of an average twenty-four-year-old male, it would probably go like this: *sex, need coffee, sex, traffic, sex, sex, what an asshole, sex, ham sandwich, sex, sex,* etc.

That's not to say that as a healthy, red-blooded woman you're not driving to work with a smile on your face some mornings reminiscing about how amazingly hot things were between the sheets the night before. But we don't seem to be prone to as much carnal contemplation as men. From an evolutionary standpoint it's the male who must go searching for a mate. In order to guarantee the propagation of the species, men are programmed to be thinking about sex and looking for it regularly.

As women, we can't change our hard wiring, but we *can* choose to think about sex more often than we do. There is, you see, a certain benefit to thinking with your panties. For one thing it's fun and also empowering. Also, conjuring up sexy images leads to arousal, and according to Laura Berman, Ph.D., a sex therapist and director of the Berman Center, the more aroused you are before sex, the easier it will be to be aroused *during* sex—and thus the easier it will be to have an orgasm. You won't be trying to go from 0 to 100 in twenty minutes or less. Or put another way, it's easier to reach a full boil if you've been simmering throughout the day.

So if you don't do it already, think with your panties. As you ride the elevator or wait for the checkout girl to ring up your purchases, revisit scorching sack sessions from your past, conjure up what sex will be like tonight with your guy, imagine your partner saying very naughty things to you, or even indulge in a sexy fantasy about the stranger in the tight jeans standing right beside you. Repeat throughout the day, especially during the hour before you'll be making love.

FORTY-FOUR

Guys Like Women Naked, Period

Every year or so at *Cosmo*, we publish an article along the lines of "How to Feel Sexier Naked." The reason we return regularly to this subject matter: As confident as young women are today, many of them still experience self-doubt about their bodies. With all the focus these days on hot celebrity bodies, you can end up feeling inadequate, especially when you strip your clothes off in front of a guy. You worry that he's checking out your love handles or butt dimples and isn't liking what he sees. Because of that worry you may refrain from strutting around the house naked or insist on keeping the lights off during a sack session. And after having sex, you may wrap yourself entirely in a sheet so that as you make your way to the bathroom, you look as if you're in a strapless wedding gown with a train.

The irony is that guys love women naked, period. From all the interviews, polls, and e-mails I've read, it's clear that they are awesomely forgiving about physical flaws, especially if they're whipped over you. Maybe it goes back to the fact that guys have fewer rods in their eyes and aren't so detail oriented (see chapter 33) or they are just overwhelmed by joy at the sheer sight of you without your clothing.

One guy summed this up brilliantly. For our fortieth birthday issue, I decided to have male writers create a page of *Cosmo* coverlines, totally from *their* perspective. Some were so funny they nearly made me cry: "Chick Flicks and Why They Can Harm Your Man," "When You Pay for Dinner, an Angel Gets Its Wings," and "Health Warning: Blue Balls Is a Real Condition—If You Deny Him Sex, He Could Die." One of the guy-written coverlines was actually a spoof on all the "How to Feel Sexier Naked" articles we'd run over time, and it was not only very funny, but it also delivered a clear perspective on the nude issue. Here's the line: "Want to Know How to Look Hot Naked? Take Your Clothes Off." That says it all: to look hot to a guy, you don't have to be perfect or drop ten pounds or go over your body with a sandblaster. You just have to strip.

Men really can't figure out what we're hung up about. They find us awesome. A guy we interviewed once about male insecurities pointed out, "Guys don't look good naked, but women almost always do."

And not only don't they get it, they find our self-consciousness a real turnoff. It's a buzz kill, they say, when a woman does the wedding wrap just to use the bathroom or won't try a position that shows off her body. If they didn't like our shape, they wouldn't be with us.

So heed what they say and flaunt it. If that's hard to do all at once, try a gradual approach. For instance, instead of leaving the lights on at first, try candlelight or soft low-watt amber or pink bulbs. Then leave the sheet on the bed and see how nice it is to walk across the room naked.

FORTY-FIVE

Guys Will Do Whatever It Takes
to Get You into Bed

I n the last few years I've learned many new, intriguing, and
reassuring things about guys. They like us (women), they
are eager to please us, and they want to know what makes
us tick. But from all the comments and e-mails I've read, I've also
seen how cold, self-serving, and manipulative some men can be.
Their blunt comments sometimes make me feel an urge to gulp,
but I also see that it's better to know than not know. Forewarned
is forearmed.

Through all the insights guys have shared about themselves,
there is one theme that leaps out again and again. Guys, particularly young guys, think about sex 24/7. They think of it when
they get up, as they go about their day, even when they look at
their sixty-year-old co-worker in her sensible pumps and blouse
with the Peter Pan collar. And because having sex is so often on
their minds, they are constantly plotting ways to get women into
bed. We once ran the following headline: "He's Scheming to Get
Laid All the Time. No, Really. All. The. Time." And that sums up
the truth perfectly.

I'm not suggesting it's a bad thing that guys work hard to bed
women. It's just smart to recognize the motives driving their behavior. One of the best stories I've heard was from a guy who, in

order to seduce a woman, pretended he had a flood in his apartment by having his roommate make a panicky call to him during dinner. Needless to say, his date suggested he stay at her place, and one thing led to another. He nicknamed the night "the *Water World* event."

Even when sex seems to be the *last* thing on a guy's mind, it isn't. Consider this innovative technique from Matt, age twenty-seven. "Oddly, the easiest way to get a woman to have sex is to take sex off the table," he told us. "Once I've convinced her that sex is not likely ('We just met, I don't usually do this'), all the pressure, expectations, and awkwardness disappear. When she's realized that what we just discussed as impossible is not only possible, but it's also happening, she's okay with it. This method is foolproof."

As I said, I'm not passing any judgment, I'm just saying *don't be fooled.*

FORTY-SIX

How Long to Wait Before Sex

I f you meet a new guy and are dying to sleep with him on the first date, don't let me stop you. You have the right to do whatever you want. Flirt with him, seduce him, take him home and bed him. But here's the rub, so to speak: you may not hear from him again.

It's totally unfair, but today, almost fifty years after the sexual revolution, some guys still react weirdly if you have sex with them "too soon." I've read the comments of lots of men on this matter, and the bottom line is, even though they do everything in their power to talk you into having sex on date one or two, on another level they often don't really want you to acquiesce to their request—that is, if they suspect there's any chance that you could be a keeper.

Why do they have this ridiculous standard? Why do they hold it against you if you sleep with them on the first or even the second date? Some of them live by a double standard that they may not be totally conscious of. They think you're slutty to cave early and some say it makes them suspect you *always* do it and therefore, they're just like every other guy to you. Others like the chase and it spoils the magic if you go to bed very early in the game.

That said, many great relationships have started with sex on the first date. The chemistry just feels right for it, and you both know that, and even if he usually adheres to a silly rule, he dismisses it because everything is perfect and the great sex that follows only confirms that it was the right thing to do. It's a gut call on your part. The only problem is that you have to be prepared for the fact that your gut might be wrong.

If you feel the least bit iffy—and you see *him* as a potential keeper—play it safe and wait until date three or four. As one guy told us, "Long, slow, torturous progress is still the hottest, healthiest scenario."

FORTY-SEVEN

How to Set His Thighs on Fire

As most women know, it doesn't take a huge amount of effort to seduce a guy. A simple phrase like "Why don't you drop your pants?" will usually suffice.

But there's seduction and then there's make-his-thighs-go-up-in-flames seduction, the kind that will have him writhing in anticipation. The latter is so much more erotic and memorable. And it actually can make the experience more physically rewarding for him, intensifying his orgasm.

Three-alarm seduction isn't difficult, but it does take some effort. You'll want to tease, tantalize, and torture him.

How to Tease:
This is where you just hint at what's going to happen so that you start a slow burn. Wear something provocative that shows plenty of skin. Bite your lip as you listen to him talk. Use suggestive language without coming right out and saying what you have in mind—like "I love it when the weather is hot and steamy like this, don't you?"

How to Tantalize:
Now turn up the heat a couple of notches. Let him know you weren't kidding with all that teasing by saying "I want you." In a whisper describe some of the naughty things you'd like to do to

him. Take his hand and run your tongue along the palm. Slip your hand between his thighs and stroke him.

How to Torture:

Prolong the burning. Rather than just falling into bed, do a striptease in which you peel away your clothes one item at a time. Or peel away *his* clothes, one piece at a time. Or give him a back rub and drag your hands over his butt and down along his hips.

Remember that even though guys always seem eager to get to the main event, taking your time really does increase his pleasure.

FORTY-EIGHT

The Kiss Men Crave the Most

I n the quest to be a fabulous lover, we sometimes lose sight of how important and powerful kissing is. You may just pay "lip service" to that part of lovemaking, rushing through it so that you and your guy can move on to pleasuring each other's more private erogenous zones. Or you may cut to the chase because you suspect your guy considers kissing to be simply a prelude to the real thing.

But indulging in lots of passionate kissing helps you build to really explosive sex. And though, yes, some men could just as easily skip it, your guy will most likely play along if you encourage it—and he will end up loving every minute of it.

What does it take to be a good kisser? Shocker of shockers, most guys don't really enjoy playing nonstop tonsil hockey. Okay, you've probably met at least a few guys who are human jackhammers, but according to every survey we've done, the majority of men like to start nice and slow with some sweet gentle kissing, building up to playful tonguing and then moving on to more intense tongue action.

Other pointers from guys: Your mouth should be as relaxed as possible, and your lips slightly moist. Key words are "tender" and "soft." When French kissing, keep your tongue fairly loose, not rigid, and think of *his* tongue as something to caress and stroke rather than jam against. As one guy once said, be an explorer, not an intruder.

FORTY-NINE

Guys Like Foreplay, Too—*Really*

uys have a reputation for liking to race through sex, skipping the foreplay and arriving as quickly as possible at the main event. That's because, unlike women, guys generally don't need much (if anything) in the way of foreplay in order to become aroused or even climax. If it's early in the relationship or a hot one-night hookup, he may be fully erect before you've even laid a hand on him. If you're entrenched in a relationship, and the newness factor is gone, you may have to help him along with a few strokes to his package. But for many guys it won't take a lot more than that to be ready for lift-off.

And yet men do enjoy foreplay, and not just because they know it's critical for their female partner and they like pleasing *her*. The more a man is fondled and stroked before intercourse, the more pleasurable the entire experience will be for him—and the more intense his orgasm may be.

So treat him to some foreplay. And don't just center all the action on his penis. He won't complain if you go there, but if you work your way there gradually and even a bit torturously, you will have him in a total lather.

You can start with very sensual kissing and then work your hands over his body. Because guys are linear in their thinking, they become hot and bothered—in a good way—if you mix it up and don't let them know what you're about to do next. Try zigzagging and lightly circling with your fingertips—and alternate that with deep kneading.

You can also focus attention on some of the surprising pleasure receptors on his body—the ears, for instance. Some guys (though not all) love it if you nibble on the outer ear, lick the rim with your tongue, and even use your tongue to probe gently inside. The neck and eyelids are also very erotic spots to kiss and lick. And don't forget to lavish attention on his nipples (see chapter 51 for those and other moan zones).

Eventually work your way south, along the pleasure trail, using circling and squiggly motions on his chest and lower abdomen and on each side of his torso. The nerves around his waist and spine and inner thighs are connected to his penis, so when you caress him there, he'll feel it *elsewhere*.

One spot that's great to key into is the place where his pubic bone is located, just below his belly button and above the beginning of his pubic hair. We call it the "almost" area because it's almost you-know-where. Lick and nibble here and he'll be writhing in anticipation.

Of course, you should expect just as much foreplay from him!

FIFTY

Men Like a Firmer Touch During Sex Than You May Suspect

You almost can't go wrong when it comes to touching a man. Guys just love having a woman's hands on them. If they have any complaint, it's that women often aren't *firm* enough with their touch.

There's a reason we females sometimes err on the side of caution. A penis can look tender, fragile even, and we may worry about hurting it. There are those horror stories, after all, about broken penises and excruciatingly painful and embarrassing trips to the ER. Who wants to be the girl responsible for *that* kind of nightmare? But though the tip of the penis is very sensitive (especially to teeth!), the skin on the rest of it is similar to forearm skin and responds well to firmness. As a guy once pointed out to us in an e-mail, "Ladies, our units aren't that sensitive. We need you to get a little rough with them—squeeze hard, suck hard, really grab onto it like you're milking a cow. You may think you're hurting him, but I guarantee if you asked him, he'd request more, more."

As for the rest of their bodies, many guys want firmness there, too. Male skin is actually twenty percent thicker than females', and so the same pressure and touch that works for you is going to be too soft for a guy. Men want you to nip their earlobes, pinch their nipples, squeeze their butts hard, make a tight ring around their penis with your fingers during oral sex, bite gently on the center part of their penis and really tug on their balls. And don't be afraid to move around in the bed. Many guys admit that they love it when there's lots of headboard banging and a few pictures dropping to the floor.

That doesn't mean that all your touches should be extra firm. Change it up. Sometimes run your fingers over his body with the tips barely touching the skin, as if you were whispering to him with your hands. Not knowing what kind of touch is coming next will totally intrigue him.

FIFTY-ONE

5 Spots (Besides the Obvious) Where a Guy Loves to Be Touched

You *know* he wants you to focus on his penis. In fact, he wants you to lavish it with manual and oral attention. But there are less obvious areas capable of providing wonderful sensations and intensifying his whole sexual experience.

1. **His nipples.** There is apparently no biological reason for men to have nipples. But a guy's are packed with nerve endings just like yours are, and they are good pleasure receptors. He may love it if you circle them with both your fingertips (moisten them first) and your tongue. Focus on the tips as well as the areolas, the pink or brown discs of skin that surround them. You can suck on his nipples, too, and some men love having them nipped or bitten. Because many women ignore this area, your guy may not be used to being touched there—so proceed gently at first.

2. **His perineum.** This is the small patch of skin between his testicles and his anus, and it's not at all the dead zone it might appear to be at a glance. It's packed with nerve endings and responds well to a slight pumping or light

rolling movement done with the knuckle of either your pointer or your middle finger. If you stimulate this area right before he ejaculates, and stay with it, it can make his orgasm stronger.

3. **The frenulum on his penis.** The frenulum is a connective fold of membrane. There's one on the underside of your tongue, for instance. There's another on the underside of a man's penis where the shaft meets the ridge that runs around the tip. Some guys experience very intense sensations when you touch it or explore it with your tongue. But because this area is, yes, packed with nerves, start gently.

4. **His butt.** Not all guys want you to go there. But there are those who love having theirs grabbed and kneaded during sex. And some guys also like you to explore their "back door" with a finger. But test the waters carefully (you might even ask, "Does this feel good for you?" as you circle the area) because back door action can freak out certain guys.

5. **His scalp.** A bit of a surprise pleasure zone, but it, too, is packed with nerve endings. When you're kissing him passionately, grab a tuft of his hair and give it a firm tug. It's an unexpected but appealing sensation.

You may have noticed that I didn't mention his testicles. They're important enough to deserve a chapter of their own (chapter 62)!

FIFTY-TWO

Guys Love a Girl on Top
(in Bed, at Least)

Overwhelmingly, the sex position guys prefer most is woman on top. Some diehards still go for missionary and around ten percent claim doggie style is their favorite, but way over half prefer to have their partners bouncing on top of them.

I know this because of the many sex surveys we've done with men. Year after year, woman on top is chosen by close to sixty percent of men as their favorite position.

Frankly, I was a little surprised the first year we did a sex survey and I learned the results. I knew from other research I'd reviewed that many *women* prefer this position—because it allows them more control in terms of the stimulation they're receiving and makes it easier for them to stimulate themselves at the same time. But I wasn't aware that it was such a huge favorite of men.

You may be sitting there snickering, thinking of course men prefer women on top—it's because they're innately lazy. True, there are some guys who *are* pretty unindustrious in the sack, and if they can lie in bed like a beached blue whale and still get off, well, that's their idea of bliss.

But that's only *some* guys. Men are hardwired so that visual cues help arouse them sexually, and many prefer the woman-on-top position because it provides great eye candy—*while* they're feeling great things, too. Also, many, many men really do want to please a woman in bed (whether it's due to generosity of spirit or a need for ego gratification or a combination of both), and they've learned from experience that women often have an easier time reaching orgasm in this position.

So if you've been shy about assuming this position, go for it. If you feel self-conscious because you'll be so *exposed*, know that guys tend to be very forgiving about any physical shortcomings women have or think they have. When you're on top, your guy is going wild gazing at your breasts, not noticing that one is slightly larger than the other. He's admiring your curves, not noticing that they're curvier than you might prefer.

To make it the most comfortable for you, start with your body almost perpendicular to his and your hands flat on the bed. As you feel more relaxed, sit up with your hands by your side.

There are a couple of variations that guys rave about. One is reverse cowgirl, which is you on top but backwards. The other is you squatting with your feet flat on the bed (rather than in a kneeling position) so that you can move up and down on him like a piston.

FIFTY-THREE

3 Secrets to Having an Orgasm

Women write into *Cosmo* asking all sorts of questions, but there is one they ask more than all the others: How can I learn to have an orgasm? Perhaps they can have one on their own but *not* during sex with a man. Or they can have one when they're making love but it's about as frequent as a total eclipse of the sun—or it doesn't occur during *intercourse* and they would really like to be able to have that happen. And some women have never had an orgasm at all.

You may have struggled with one of these issues yourself. Studies show that without accompanying manual stimulation of the clitoris, only twenty-five percent of women experience orgasm often or very often during intercourse. Five to ten percent of women have never had an orgasm at all.

It just seems so unfair. Relatively few men have trouble in this department—in fact, one of the biggest sexual glitches among younger men is that they orgasm too *quickly*. You can't help but wonder why nature made it this tough for women. One recent theory, by biologist Dr. Elizabeth Lloyd, holds that female orgasm is elusive because it doesn't have an evolutionary function. Women can have intercourse and become pregnant without climaxing, so it's not necessary for the survival of the species. In her book *The Case of the Female Orgasm: Bias in the Science of Evolution*, Dr. Lloyd theorizes that females developed the nerve pathways for orgasm simply because they had the same body plan as males during the first weeks of life in the womb. The clitoris, she says, is vestigial in women—just like nipples in men.

Regardless of the fact that the female orgasm may have no evolutionary purpose and despite the fact that orgasm can be elusive, you can absolutely improve your ability to climax, to climax more regularly, and to climax during sex with your partner. Over the past few years I've read an awful lot on this subject and three basic strategies are key to success.

1. First and foremost you have to be the *boss* of your own orgasms. Many women tend to see this as the *guy's* responsibility, and when it doesn't happen, they either blame him for being a lousy lover or blame their own bodies for not responding. Just think of the terminology you hear women use: when they *do* have an orgasm, they say things like "He made me come."

   Men, on the other hand, always take charge of their own pleasure. Granted, it's a piece of cake for most of them, and they certainly rely on a woman to arouse and stimulate them during sex, but at the same time they're always making sure the job is getting done. For instance, a guy may pick up the speed of his thrusting during intercourse in order to make sure he reaches the finish line. Or he may indulge in a little fantasy during sex just to keep the moment hot.

   So that's the first thing you need to do: think more like a guy. Tell yourself that you're the boss of your orgasms and that you are going to do what it takes to climax.

2. But let's not get to sex with a man quite yet. In order to

climax when you're making love, you need to first know how to do it on your own. By pleasuring *yourself*. If you've been there and done that, just skim or skip this section. But many women admit in e-mails to *Cosmo* that they have never masturbated. They've felt too embarrassed to try it, or unsure about what to do—or worse, ashamed because of some kind of religious training or parent-inspired inhibitions.

But if you've never masturbated, it's time to let go of your hang-ups. Masturbating is a normal, healthy activity, even for women in steady relationships, and for most women it's the way they learn to orgasm during sex. So dim the lights, put on some music, even light a few candles, and get ready to explore your own body.

Though you can start by stroking your entire body, ultimately you need to focus on one tiny area: your clitoris. It's the bundle of nerve endings with a little hood about two inches in front of your vagina. Though some women do achieve orgasm through stimulation of their G-spots (an area inside the vagina), the clitoris is the key spot for most.

On the other hand, there is no stimulation technique that works across the board for all women. You may have to test out a variety of moves before you find the winning formula.

How do you start? Most women use the tips of one or two fingers to gently rub or massage the clitoris in little circles. One woman wrote in to tell us that by accident she had discovered that touching the left side of her clitoris made all the difference. More than one reader we've interviewed for articles has said that direct manual stimulation feels too intense and they prefer to rub with their underwear between their clitoris and their fingers. And many women discover that a vibrator or handheld water nozzle enables them to achieve just the right amount of stimulation.

Don't get discouraged if nothing happens right away. It may require several sessions for you to feel relaxed enough. Plus, you should know that it takes the average woman twenty minutes to reach the orgasmic platform, the point when orgasm is almost a foregone conclusion. If everything is proceeding okay, you will start to feel a growing tingling sensation. From there, the more you just relax and let go, the greater your chances of climaxing.

3. Once you know your own personal formula, you can take it to bed with a man. But you have to let him in on it. Many women feel awkward doing that. They think it'll make them look pushy, or they're embarrassed because their personal formula will seem a little quirky. But it's clear to me from all the interviews we've done that the good guys want more than anything to please a woman, and they aren't put off by individualistic requests. They experience too big of a rush from seeing you have an orgasm.

So during foreplay, show him what you like. In a survey, sixty-five percent of guys said that when a woman actually demonstrated the moves that pleased her, they thought it was hot and it enabled them to learn her preferences. You can even place his hand over yours while you're doing it so he gets a real sense of your technique.

If a vibrator is the secret to your success, you may want to introduce it to your lovemaking. Afraid that will turn him off? In a survey, almost sixty percent of guys said that they'd be psyched if their girlfriend brought one to bed. Just over thirty percent said they'd be a little uneasy but would be willing to give it a try.

If your partner is a pretty skilled lover and is enthusiastic about manual and oral stimulation, you can try without any direct assistance from yourself. But you still need to let him know what feels the best. You don't want to sound like the navigational system in a car, but you can convey your response by moaning or saying, "That feels amazing." Sometimes it's not technique that needs to be addressed, it's timing. Remember the twenty-minute factor. Guys don't need as much foreplay and thus some have a tendency to rush things. You need to let your guy know that you need more time.

What about climaxing during intercourse? Some women are able to but for many it's a challenge. Again, clitoral stimulation is key, but during intercourse there's not always the right degree of contact between the penis and the clitoris. Many women solve this problem by stimulating themselves manually during intercourse. Over and over again readers tell us that they like the woman-on-top position, because it's easy to engage in manual stimulation at the same time—they do it or their guy does it with his thumb. This position can also allow the penis to come into direct contact with the clitoris. One woman we interviewed said that she leaned forward with her arms bent as though she were about to do a push-up so her body made a forty-five-degree angle with her boyfriend's chest. It put the ideal amount of pressure on her clitoris. After just minutes of rocking her pelvis back and forth against him, she climaxed.

Some women can also have an orgasm from stimulation of their G-spots, a dime-size area on the front wall of the vagina. Your partner can reach it by inserting his finger in a hooked position and massaging or pumping. Certain sex positions, like doggie style or girl-on-top, also can facilitate a G-spot orgasm.

Keep in mind, though, that if you can't achieve an orgasm through intercourse, you shouldn't torture yourself. As I already pointed out, many women never do, and every sex expert will tell you that all orgasms are great, no matter how they happen.

FIFTY-FOUR

And If Those Don't Work . . .
9 Extra Little Orgasm Tricks

If you follow the steps in the previous chapter, you will hopefully have success in climaxing during sex. But if it hasn't happened, don't despair. Many women report that, though the basic moves help get them close, it often takes one final little twist or flourish—sometimes even a quirky one—to take them over the edge. Think of it as creating your own orgasm cocktail. One or more of these may work for you.

1. **Exercise your PC muscles.** By now you've probably heard about your PC (short for pubococcygeus) muscles. They are pelvic muscles that when contracted stop the flow of urine. But they also play a role in your sexual life. The stronger they are, the more blood pumps through them and the easier it is for you to become aroused during sex.

   But that's not all these little devils can do. When contracted during intercourse, they provide a tighter grip on your man's penis. Final bonus: many women find that contracting them during sex makes it easier for them to climax.

   To keep your pelvic muscles strong, you need to perform Kegel exercises, named for the doctor who invented them. Kegels are a simple series of contractions of your PC muscles. If you aren't sure where they are, use this technique: when you are about to pee, try stopping—but without engaging the muscles in your thighs, butt, or abdomen. Sounds tricky but you'll figure it out. Now, to do Kegels, squeeze your PC muscles tight for ten seconds (you may have to work up to it) and then release. Repeat three or four times. Do several times a day. The fun thing is that you can do them anywhere. To keep you in the habit, pick specific times to practice them—like when you're in the shower, or making your smoothie in the blender, or driving home from work.

2. **Use lube.** This is a suggestion I first heard from sex therapist Dr. Laura Berman; she says that vaginal lubricant is a secret orgasm weapon. It creates a slickness that allows you to better concentrate on all the sensations you're feeling down there.

3. **Adjust the angle of your legs.** According to Felice Dunas, Ph.D., author of *Passion Play: Ancient Secrets for a Lifetime of Health and Happiness Through Sensational Sex,* in general it's easier for women to orgasm if their knees are below their hips. She suggests that you put a pillow under your butt or lie on the edge of the bed with your legs dangling during missionary-style sex. The theory: this will increase the tension in your groin muscles, which stimulates the nerves in your pelvic region.

4. **Take long, deep breaths from your pelvic area.** It immediately intensifies anything you're feeling down there.

5. **Breathe in synch with *him*.** For some reason your body

just totally relaxes when you do that, and you can really feel things down there.

6. **Lean your head over the side of the bed.** This is a technique suggested by Aurelie Jones Goodwin, a psychologist and co-author of *A Woman's Guide to Overcoming Sexual Fear and Pain.* She says that researchers have found that tightening and releasing large muscle groups triggers orgasm, and stretching the neck muscle is particularly good.

7. **Turn your brain off.** A Dutch study that scanned the brains of women during orgasm found that the parts of the brain responsible for such emotions as anxiety and fear went blank for up to two minutes (men, on the other hand, seemed to be using their brains to interpret the experience). The researchers believe that the results explain why women need to be relaxed in order to climax. If their anxiety level is high, they can't turn their brains off.

8. **Have him try stimulating your clitoris a whole different way** than he usually does. A reader told us that having her guy use his tongue in a figure-eight design on her clitoris was what took her over the edge. Another said that having her boyfriend push on her like a doorbell was the ticket.

9. **Get a Brazilian wax.** I don't have any evidence this works but I thought I'd throw it in since actress Eva Longoria swore by it when we interviewed her. She said that being nearly bare down there intensifies sensations. "It makes sex better, orgasm-wise," she revealed. She claimed the difference between having sex with a Brazilian and without was comparable to the difference between rubbing your arm and gently tapping it.

FIFTY-FIVE

How to Be Great in Bed

Though there's a lot of emphasis these days on how important it is for a man to understand the complexities of a woman's body and what it really takes to please her in bed, women want to know how to be fantastic lovers themselves. Who doesn't want to think that as her guy is lying next to her in a postcoital daze, the only thought drifting through his brain is *Damn, that's the best sex I've ever had.*

When we ask men to describe what makes a woman good in bed, the same three factors turn up again and again: (1) skill, (2) a willingness to mix it up, incorporating lots of variety, and (3) good old-fashioned enthusiasm, a passion for what you're doing.

That's not as daunting of a list as it may seem at first. If you bought a book called *You on Top*, then you're obviously enthusiastic on the subject of sex, so you've got that one covered already. For the other two it really comes down to experience. As the actor Matt Dillon summed up so succinctly when we interviewed him, "I believe people who have more sex are better at sex." (And you can accelerate the experience process by having a partner who is a good teacher and a willing explorer.)

But there's something else, I think, that can make you not only a good lover but one who leaves a guy weak in the knees simply anticipating a sack session with you: developing your own little signature sex move. I'm not talking so much about being fabulous at a *particular* skill—like oral sex—but rather performing one fairly small move that's so erotically unique and different from what he's experienced before that it totally captivates him. Think of it as a "sextra"—adding an extra spin or twist to what's already in your sexual repertoire. When we talk to guys about sex, they always wax poetic about the sextras they've experienced.

You don't want to do anything scary or ridiculous. A reader once wrote in to say that she loved to pull her boyfriend into the shower with her and massage his penis with hair conditioner. Unless he planned to wear his penis in a sleek ponytail later, that sounded pretty inane to me.

For your consideration, here are a few examples of quirky signature moves that some guys find totally thrilling and unforgettable:

- Going down on him when he's on all fours.
- Making a tight ring with your thumb and forefinger around the base of his penis, forming a second ring around the head, and then going up with one hand and down with the other.
- Pulling his pants down and pleasuring him while his pants are around his ankles and he can't get away.
- Squeezing his nipples right before he climaxes.
- Taking him in your mouth and then swirling your tongue around like a pencil sharpener.
- Starting a hand job by running a fingertip down his butt crack, over his testicles, and up his penis.
- Pulling his butt into you as he thrusts.

FIFTY-SIX

Guys Have Sex Fears, Too

You know that obnoxious little audiotape that can run through your head when you first have sex with a guy? The one that asks questions like *Does he like the way I look? Does he notice the stretch marks on my boobs? Do I smell okay?* The one that won't turn off even when you tell it to?

Well, men have audiotapes, too. It's hard to imagine any self-doubt or self-loathing coursing through their brains because they seem so confident, even cocky, but it's there, repeating miserable messages. One twenty-something guy we interviewed summed it up so well. "I want to be a sex god," he confided, "but in my head I'm thinking, *What if the last guy she slept with was bigger? What if I can't get it up? What if I can't get her off?* The pressure is insane."

It's not your job to coddle him or play therapist. But you can make the sexual experience even better for him if you help him feel good about his performance.

What's key is to avoid hyperbole. Guys see right through it. Short, casual, and slightly wicked-sounding remarks work best. Several guaranteed pleasers:

- "You feel so big inside me."
- "Wow, where did you learn *that*?"
- "I've never been touched like that before, but it feels great."

FIFTY-SEVEN

12 Oral Sex Tricks That Will Make Him Putty in Your Hands (Send Him to the Moon)

One of the questions I hear frequently in my job via reader e-mail is, "What's the secret to great oral sex?" Women know that guys crave being pleased that way, and so they want to learn how to master the art, thus searing in their man's brain forever how good they are. They realize it's tricky business, though, and they're afraid they may be making mistakes—like hurting the guy with their teeth—or being too tentative. Guys aren't much help when it comes to perfecting one's skills. They're so grateful for your participation that they don't want to put a damper on things by making any suggestions or hinting that what you're doing isn't brilliant.

But guys do speak to *us*, and over the years I've heard these helpful suggestions for perfecting the art:

1. The number one secret to great oral sex is enthusiasm. If you look and act like you're loving it, it's almost (though not quite) enough to blow his mind.

2. Take a little time getting to where the main action is—it will build up anticipation and intensify the whole thing for him. Run your tongue down his pleasure trail—that area

from his belly button to his groin, and also along the inside of his thighs. Stroke gently with your hands as you go.

3. *Blow* is really the wrong word. Oral sex doesn't involve any blowing—unless you want to tantalize him with a few breaths on his penis before you start. What you should be doing is licking and sucking. While licking, use both the tip of your tongue and the whole surface (including the rough underside) and also alternate pressure. The tip of his penis is more tender than the middle of the shaft, so treat each area accordingly. While sucking, it's important to be careful with your teeth, keeping them tucked behind your lips.

4. Don't make all the activity just about your lips. Guys report that some women simply move the penis back and forth through their lips. Let him experience your whole mouth. Move it back and forth in there. Change the angle of your mouth.

5. Don't stop using your tongue once you take him into your mouth. Run it up and down the shaft. Flick it back and forth.

6. Use your hands, too. One guy once said that extraordinary oral sex is "like holding a baseball bat—it requires both hands." You can also use one hand to make a ring around the base of his penis and squeeze a little. He may also like it if you tug on his balls, squeeze his butt, or knead his perineum (see chapter 51).

7. Hum or moan while you're doing it. He'll feel interesting vibrations.

8. Don't forget to spend some time licking and sucking gently on his testicles.
9. Put a pillow under his head so he can watch.
10. Lock eyes with him while you're doing it.
11. Try it when he's standing. Supposedly more blood rushes to his groin then and everything will become more intense for him.
12. As for swallowing, that's your decision. But whether you do or not, guys complain that some women don't stay with the whole process long enough. They reduce intensity too soon into orgasm.

FIFTY-EIGHT

9 Unexpected and
Very Sexy Sensations to Try in Bed

1. Suck on a breath mint before going down on him. The mentholated flavor in your mouth will create a tingly sensation.
2. Run an ice cube over his torso and thighs.
3. Take an old strand of fake pearls or other beads and, holding each end, pull it back and forth around the shaft of his penis.
4. Very lightly run your fingertips over his entire body as if your fingers were feathers.
5. Take a sip of hot water—as hot as you can stand—before going down on him, and then, keeping your mouth closed, swish it all around his penis.
6. Stroke his penis while wearing silk gloves.
7. Chill a bunch of marbles in the fridge. Toss them on the bed and make him lie on them while you straddle him.
8. Gently drag a cashmere scarf along his naked body.
9. When he's face down, rub your breasts along his back and butt.

FIFTY-NINE

How to Have the Most Sensual Sex in the World

There are lots of different kinds of sex a couple can have: everything from lazy-rainy-Sunday-afternoon lovemaking to a fun, feisty romp to totally animalistic sex. You may prefer one type to another and so may your partner, but your relationship will stay spicy if you rely on a whole menu and don't simply resort to your favorite and his.

One of the great kinds of sex is sensuous, slow-burn sex, or what sometimes gets called "soulful sex"—it's intense and charged but not hurried. Women tend to love soulful sex because it can be so intimate. Though it may not turn up at the very top of many guys' lists, they can easily discover the pluses: when a couple takes it slow, there's often a bigger, more explosive physical payoff at the end—for both of them! It just may be up to you to lead him in that direction by setting the stage. In some ways you'll be borrowing a page from Tantric sex, which encourages a very slow buildup of arousal to guarantee not only amazing pleasure but also a spiritual experience. The problem is that Tantric sex supposedly requires *hours* of a couple's time. Think of this as sort of *modified* Tantric. You want to commit at least an hour to it but not the entire weekend! Here are some guidelines.

- Ambiance is critical with sensuous, slow-burn sex. Make sure your bedroom or wherever you're planning to make love is free of clutter or anything that will prevent you from feeling calm and relaxed. Light candles (though you'll need to remember to blow them out if you go to sleep afterwards!) and even incense (sandalwood, frankincense, and musk are all very exotic scents). If music won't be too distracting, play a few sexy CDs. Or for an enchanting change of pace, play one of those CDs of thunderstorm, ocean, or rain forest sounds.

- Set the pace before you're in the bedroom by engaging in a languorous but erotic activity together. Enjoy wine and cheese, especially a really rich and buttery cheese (like triple-crème Brie) or runny cheese (like Vacherin du Jura). Or shampoo each other's hair. (If you have any doubts about how erotic this can be, watch Robert Redford doing it for Meryl Streep in *Out of Africa*.)

- Get naked and sit cross-legged across from each other and then spend a minute or so just locking eyes, without touching. Some guys find this too intense, but if he's game, it can be a very sexy and intimate experience.

- Start touching, but just each other's hands and arms first. Very lightly run your fingers along the underside of his wrists and the V-shaped areas between his fingers. Trail your fingers up and down his arms. Some guys love it if you also do this to their armpits (go figure). Ask him to do the same to you.

- Kiss, but let your kisses be just as slow as everything else you're doing.

- Use your hands to explore other areas of his body—except

his most private areas. Run your fingers over his face, arms, torso, and legs, barely touching him—as if your fingers were feathers. Let him do the same to you.

- Now slowly move to each other's hot zones. Using a scented oil, caress his penis slowly and deliberately. Place both hands around the shaft, one above the other and pull one hand off, then the other and start all over again. And don't forget to caress his testicles. He should use the scented oil on you, too, not only massaging the outer area of your vagina, but also letting his fingers explore inside of you very slowly.

- When you're ready for intercourse, try it sitting up with you in his lap. Lock eyes again.

- Synchronize your breathing to his. It's not only very intimate but it's been shown to improve a woman's chance of having an orgasm.

SIXTY

Guys Secretly Love a Little Kinkiness

Remember the episode of *Desperate Housewives* in which the now-dead husband of Marcia Cross's character confesses that he loves to be hog-tied and dominated during sex? After the show, a friend of mine who's single again and dating confessed, "That's my worst nightmare—to meet some fabulous guy and discover that he has this really kinky side to him—like he'd love to wear my panties when we're having sex or he can only have an orgasm if I grind a stiletto into his chest."

Some guys do have very serious fetishes and kinky needs, but they're in the minority. Most guys have fairly straightforward tastes, needing just your presence and some perfunctory stimulation in order to be blissed out in bed. . . . And *yet*, that said, many guys crave just a *little* bit of kinkiness—kinky lite, if you will. No, they don't necessarily want to wear your thong, but they love the idea of the taboo, of experimenting and breaking the so-called rules once in a while, just to spice things up. When we polled five thousand male readers and asked them, "What's the one thing you're dying for a girl to do (even though you don't really expect her to do it)?" thirty-five percent checked "Invite a beautiful stranger over for a three-way." You may assume your guy would have no interest in any of this, but that could be simply because he's never confessed to it. Many guys are too nervous or sheepish to ever suggest anything risqué. The status quo works well enough, so they stay silent—but ever hopeful.

So where does this leave you? Maybe *you'd* like to break the rules, too—not necessarily drag a strange chick named Tara into the sack with you and your guy, but stretch the boundaries a little. Or on the other hand, maybe the word *taboo* strikes terror into your heart.

Well, you can offer your guy a *sense* of the taboo without having to cross any major borders. All it takes is a little experimenting. Especially if you surprise him. Guys get a rush when they realize you are headed someplace new but they aren't sure where. And the great thing is that *you'll* probably find a little experimenting invigorating, too.

A few ideas: Blindfold him one night and tell him to do nothing while you pleasure him—other than experience the tactile sensations; strip his clothes off in the kitchen and make love to him on the floor; grab one of his ties, hide it under a pillow in bed, and before he knows what's up, bind his hands together and lace the tie through the headboard; give him a lap dance; play-act and pretend you're a hot stranger he's just met.

Like I said, he'll absolutely love the novelty and experimentation. And no one named Tara has to step foot in your bedroom.

SIXTY-ONE

How to *Double* a Man's Pleasure in Bed

arlier I mentioned that guys like a firmer touch in bed than women may imagine. But there's another touching technique that can really captivate, as well. You could call it double delight.

The basic idea is that you stimulate *two* body parts at the same time—kind of a stereo effect. For instance, as you trace your tongue around the rim of your guy's ear, you can run your fingers seductively along the inside of his thigh. This technique is ultra-pleasurable not only because you're in contact with more flesh but also because you're triggering twice the erotic anticipation.

There's a twist that makes it even more delicious. Use the *identical* stroke on each body part. You could, for example, make circles with your tongue on his nipples at the same time that you stroke his testicles in a circular motion. There's something about experiencing the same exact movement in two places simultaneously that is truly mind-blowing.

SIXTY-TWO

The Most Neglected Moan Zone
on a Man's Body

E very time we have ever done a survey and asked guys what body part they wish women would lavish more attention on in bed, we always hear the same comment from the majority of them: *their balls*. Reports of such oversight also turn up when we do roundups of guys asking them about their most pleasurable sexual experiences. At least a few guys mention how nice it is when a woman doesn't ignore their "twins" or "jewels."

Why do women give this particular body part short shrift? Maybe because a man's testicles never appear very demanding—they just kind of hang there listlessly while the penis is standing up straight, begging for attention. Or maybe because they seem so delicate, like two little quail eggs, and we're afraid to handle them.

But the testicles are almost as erotically charged as the penis, and men love to have theirs touched, especially when you're touching the penis at the same time. And a man's balls aren't nearly as fragile as they look. Fondle them, rub them gently with a warm wet washcloth, lick them, use your tongue to trace a W on the outside of the sac, take them gingerly in your mouth, and don't even be afraid to lightly tug on them, especially when he starts to orgasm.

SIXTY-THREE

You *Can* Get a Man to Please You in Bed

We excerpt lots of sexy romances and thrillers in *Cosmo* and with every one of them there are two things you can be absolutely sure of: The guy will turn out to be enormously endowed, often causing the woman to gasp in surprise at the size. And he will know exactly how to bring her to orgasm the first time they have sex. The same thing happens in the movies. A couple rip off each other's clothes, drop into bed, and before long the chick is screaming in ecstasy.

But that's not the way it generally works in real life. For starters, even some of the most wonderful guys in the world haven't yet become clued in to the nuances of pleasing a woman sexually. Says social philosopher Michael Gurian, author of *The Wonder of Boys*: "A lot of young men are unaware that the majority of women don't have vaginal orgasms, but in fact need clitoral stimulation. I can't tell you how many men I've had to explain this to in my family therapist practice. Women have to educate men about this."

Even if you're dating a guy who is basically a good lover, initially he may not know the type of stimulation that works for you. Women are very different in how they like to be touched. Your new guy's previous girlfriend may have had a whole different set of criteria.

The comforting news: most guys want nothing more than to be educated by the women they're sleeping with.

The best strategy for doing that is not to make a huge deal out of it. Just as when you're trying to get him to open up, be casual and concrete.

Gurian says that an easy-going, clear approach is with body language. "Guide him physically," he says. "For instance, if his tongue is missing your clitoris, touch his head lightly to move it one way or the other. He'll sense he's doing something wrong and ask what to do better, or the physical contact will solve the problem."

When he gets it right, offer plenty of reinforcement—as in moaning. Later, you can even mention the specific thing he did and say how amazing it was—not, says Gurian, as if you were getting into a "talk" but in the way you might share a naughty secret with him. As in, "When you touched me that way, I was afraid you might have to peel me off the ceiling."

And what if your guy knows how to please you but is lazy or doesn't always feel he has to reciprocate, especially with oral sex? "Appeal to his sense of fairness," stresses Gurian. "Deep down men want to be fair, so insist on balance."

SIXTY-FOUR

5 Mind-Blowing Sex Tricks

O ne of the biggest challenges I thought I'd face in my job was coming up with fresh, inventive sex tips month after month. Sex is such a basic, primal activity—after a while what can you possibly do that's new? And yet just as food is reinvented repeatedly by great chefs, sex is reinvented regularly— not only by sex experts but also by gutsy, experimental couples everywhere.

Here are five tricks that just stand out from the pack:

- When fondling your man's penis, slip a hair scrunchy around the base of it. The tight scrunchy combined with your touch creates an amazing sensation.
- Gather four pillows under your butt before he enters you in the missionary position. The angle this creates adds a new twist and guarantees better contact between his penis and your clitoris. Plus, there's something thrilling about floating up there on all those pillows.
- When you're on top, pull up your knees and then rock side-to-side as he thrusts. Or move your hips in a swirling motion.
- Using a bit of lube, make two fists around the shaft of his penis and twist in opposite directions.

- Slip a glazed doughnut around his penis and nibble it off. In his book *I Am Charlotte Simmons*, novelist Tom Wolfe mocked our write-up of this move. But perhaps he was just jealous no one had ever tried it on him.

SIXTY-FIVE

How to Keep Your Sex Life Red Hot

As hard as it may be to face, there comes a time in every relationship when the hot sex you were having in the early days starts to cool down. That's not to say it evolves into the kind of sex you'd expect from the couple played by Bonnie Hunt and Steve Martin in the *Cheaper by the Dozen* movies, but it's probably less frequent, less crazy, less earsplitting than it used to be. No one's calling the cops anymore when you two hit the sheets. This happens to just about every couple—including the ones who are *all over* each other when they sit across from you at dinner parties. Even Demi Moore and Ashton Kutcher reached a point when they clearly didn't tear each other's clothes off the second they walked in the door (you know this because a year into their relationship Demi said in an interview that *sometimes* they liked to sit around naked and watch Court TV).

There are actually a few pluses to the cooling down that comes with relationship sex versus infatuation sex. It gives you a chance to explore *soulful* sex, where you really connect on a deeper level (see chapter 59). Also, since early sex is sometimes a little on the clunky side even while being hot, you can work out any kinks— reinforce with him how you like to be pleasured, for instance, and learn what he likes best.

That said, cooled-down sex can be, well, a letdown. Your feelings for each other are probably growing stronger, but you can't help but miss the heat and even wonder if it suggests there's a problem. Happily, there's a way to increase the steaminess.

One of the key moves you need to make is reintroduce the notion of novelty—which is what made things so damn exciting to begin with. In chapter 41, I mentioned how anthropologist Helen Fisher said that adding novelty to relationships increases dopamine, which in turn increases feelings similar to infatuation. Novelty can do the same for your sex life, too. You need to break out of any ruts you've fallen into, introduce at least a few new "spices." It may never be the exact firestorm you experienced in the beginning, but there can still be scorch marks on your mattress.

Start by asking yourself the following questions.

When was the last time you:

- Had sex standing up?
- Had sex in a different room other than your bedroom?
- Had sex outside?
- Brought a sex toy or a prop to bed?
- Had a quickie during which you just slid your panties to the side rather than took them off?
- Switched positions at least three times during sex?
- Tried a totally *new* position?
- Filled the bedroom with twenty-five lit candles before you made love?
- Brought food to bed?
- *Scheduled* sex because you both have been crazy busy and you didn't want to go too long without it?
- Grabbed your guy from behind in the kitchen and dragged him off to the bedroom?

- Had really long sex, as in longer than thirty minutes?
- Made up a private sexy game? Like a dice game in which each number rolled represents something you must do to each other.
- Were blindfolded during sex? Or blindfolded him?
- Used lube?
- Wore really hot lingerie to bed?
- Tied his hands to the bed or had him tie yours?
- Looked at a sex book or article for ideas?
- Used an idea you found in a sex book or article?
- Made a sex tape together?
- Shared your fantasies with each other?
- Each wrote down on paper things you'd love done to you, put them in a bowl, and took turns drawing them out?
- Made sex a whole-evening adventure: bath, mutual massage, bedside champagne . . . ?
- Read the Kama Sutra?
- Told him to be in charge so you could completely let go?
- Told him to let go completely and allow you to be in charge?

If the answer to most is more than a few weeks (or even *never*), you're probably stuck in a rut. So let the questions themselves inspire you to change that.

SIXTY-SIX

Sex Is One of the Best Things in Life

My job involves covering lots of different subjects: fashion, beauty, celebrities, men, love, relationships, health, personal growth, news issues for women—and of course sex. It's not an overwhelming part of our coverage, but it's vital to the mix and we tackle the subject more candidly than any other woman's magazine.

So because of this I read an awful lot about sex and think about it as a subject probably more than at any other time in my life.

And what this regular focus on the subject does is constantly remind me how good sex is for us. Helen Gurley Brown once told me that "sex is one of the three best things out there, and I don't even remember what the other two are." I wouldn't necessarily go that far, but I know what she means. Sex *is* a wonderful, magical thing. It not only leads to amazing physical pleasure and release, but it's also a way to establish a remarkable intimacy with another person. It's part of the glue that bonds you to your partner in a romantic relationship.

None of this is news to women in their twenties who read the magazine or come to work for me. Many of them are in new relationships with plenty of sexual heat. They also view sex as a healthy part of life, without the hang-ups that some baby boomers have.

But let's face it. Even those of us who love sex and know how key it is for a relationship fall into bad habits. You get too tired for sex or too stressed out for sex and it becomes less of a priority. You might make the mistake of thinking that irregular sex is okay because the two of you are still snuggling and cuddling and things between you seem just fine. But there's every chance that your guy doesn't like the fall-off. Unfortunately guys don't speak up about it or else they deliver the message in code (a guy once told us in an interview that when men say "We should stay in more," it really means "We should have more sex"). Granted, more and more I hear complaints from women saying that their guys don't want sex as much as they do, but in general guys want a regular diet of it.

And even if you think you're comfortable with less sex, it may really be because of extenuating circumstances. Perhaps sex has become hurried or not as tender as it once was and that leaves you less than eager.

If sex is now a low priority or doesn't feel like one of the best things in life anymore, think about why. Is your bedroom so piled with junk that it's not inspiring seduction? Do a cleanup and try adding the color blue or turquoise—experts say they create a sensuous vibe. Are you truly bushed at the end of the day? Try sex before dinner.

When we interviewed the charming and gorgeous Patrick Dempsey, who plays "Dr. McDreamy" on *Grey's Anatomy*, he had a few illuminating thoughts from a man's point of view. "It's important to have a lot of sex because if you don't, your relationship will definitely be in danger," he told us. "I think you have to have great, hot sex, and you have to experiment with your partner. . . . That's what is going to keep you together. If you stop having sex, your relationship is over."

I guess we should consider that doctor's orders.

PART FIVE

YOU ON TOP

Style

SIXTY-SEVEN

How to Have Style

There are several pluses to having a fashion department at a magazine besides the beautiful pages they produce each month. For one, as they're considering what fashion or look to shoot for a particular issue, they call in tons of sample clothes and hang them on racks out in a hallway. It's a great preview of what you should be buying for the next season, though there's always a little swell of panic when you realize that the new look is boho or mod or classic and you don't have one solitary item like that in your closet.

I also find it intriguing to spend time with fashion editors and stylists because they're very different from people on the "writing" or articles side of magazines, which is the area *I* started in. These editors are just *obsessed* with clothes. Not long after I began at *Cosmo*, we were pulling together a story on actresses as the next supermodels and someone suggested Minnie Driver. "No way," one of the fashion editors said. "She's worn the same coat five times lately, and just for *that*, she shouldn't qualify." Poor Minnie, I remember thinking. That's how seriously these people take fashion.

They also always look incredibly cool. They cover fashion for a living, so of course they know what the trends are, but I think great style really comes naturally to most of them. If it *doesn't* come naturally to you, you can probably never dress with the same flair and ease as they do, but I think there are a few strategies you can crib from them:

- They always buy killer shoes and boots. I have never known a fashion editor who wasn't a shoe slut, and they generally splurge on amazing-looking designer shoes (like Manolas and Prada)—even the young editors who aren't making much money yet. Now this might seem flighty, but they don't necessarily buy a ton of shoes. They pick up a few great pairs that are versatile enough to wear again and again. They seem to live by the philosophy that the right footwear can make an entire outfit come together or give a real kick to something that's a little on the plain side. For instance, if you add a pair of awesome cowboy boots to jeans and a tank top, you suddenly have a drop-dead outfit.
- They find the lines that really work for them and stick with them, even as the trends change. By "lines" I mean the shapes—for instance, slim pants or flowy tops or pencil skirts. When you follow this strategy you not only ensure that you're always in something that flatters you—because it may show off your great boobs or legs—but you also develop a look over time that people associate with you.

  If you think about the celebs with great style, they tend to stay with a certain silhouette. Liz Hurley, for instance. Everything she owns is fairly nipped in at the waist: You'd never see her in anything flowy or Grecian-style.

  How do you know which lines work best for you? If you put something on and the minute you look in the mirror you have a sense that it works, then it probably does. If you find yourself stepping back, twirling, staring and endlessly wondering, there may be something not quite right about it. Rachel Zoe, the celebrity stylist who writes a column for us, says that another way to tell is to pay attention to what people compliment. There's probably a common denominator to the shapes that draw raves again and again.

- They spend money on classic pieces—like a perfect black pencil skirt or pair of light wool pants. Because they're going to wear them again and again—and for several years—they want them to be great. Good design and good fabric are worth the money in this case.

- They buy a few trendy pieces to wear each season, but they never overdo it. They might buy a flowy top in a neutral color and mix it with different bottoms. Then they're not stuck with a closetful of fads at the end of a season.

- They are never, ever matchy-matchy. You know how newspaper reporters go to jail rather than reveal a source? Well, a fashion editor would rather serve time than put together an outfit with too many hits of the same color.

    Freelance fashion stylist Ariel Laurence, whom I love to work with, says red shoes paired with a red jacket is just too much, for instance. But if the jacket has a tiny line of red, then red shoes could work. Even better: red shoes with a gray or brown suit! Less is always more.

- They buy a great designer bag every year. And a great coat. Because you wear them everywhere. And they make a great statement.

SIXTY-EIGHT

When You Should
Always Wear Stilettos

I f you ever have to really strut your stuff and make a knock-out impression, do not attempt it in flat shoes or nice, boring pumps. Put on a killer pair of high heels. They'll make you feel sexier, more sophisticated, more confident—and more powerful.

I became convinced of the merit of this after attending my first *Cosmo* cover shoot. I had been working at the magazine for a few months before I was able to escape from the office long enough to head downtown in Manhattan and experience the whole cover thing in action. I'd been on plenty of photo shoots over the years—not only as an editor but also, in my twenties, as a model—so I basically knew what to expect. But I figured a *Cosmo* cover shoot was probably going to be a lot more thrilling.

And it *was*. In fact, it was very close to the way magazine cover shoots look in movies and TV shows—people buzzing around like bees from a trampled hive, the makeup artist and hairstylist constantly fussing over the model (in this case it was a fashion model, not an actress), and the photographer shouting, "Fantastic, that's perfect, give that to me again, fantastic," as he clicked away.

And I learned something new that day. I noticed that the model picked out a great pair of stilettos to wear with each outfit—despite the fact that our covers cut off the model at about mid-thigh and you don't see her lower legs, let alone her feet.

"The models all do that," my design director, Ann Kwong, told me when I inquired about it. "They go for the highest pair of heels the stylist has."

"How come?" I asked.

"When you're in heels, it forces you up on your tippytoes," she said. "You're more erect, and since it pushes your torso out, you look sexier and more elegant. But it's not just the look. All that height gives them a feeling of power."

As I considered her comment, I knew she was right. Of course, you don't want heels so high that you fall on your butt as you walk across a prospective employer's office or while you're giving a kiss to the guy you're on a second date with. But if you want to impress, if you want to feel as if *you're* totally in charge of the situation, go for as much height as your legs can handle.

SIXTY-NINE

The Best Tricks I Learned
from Fashion Stylists

You are probably aware of that breed of people known as celebrity fashion stylists. They're the ones who dress celebs for the red carpet and, in some cases, really define a star's whole style. That's what the amazing Rachel Zoe has done for Lindsay Lohan and Nicole Ritchie.

Fashion stylists are hired for most magazine photo shoots, too, even if it's just a portrait. The stylist calls in the appropriate clothes and then makes them fit right and look good by doing everything from steaming them to tightening baggy items in the back with clips that resemble clothes pins. If the clothes are too small, rather than too big, the stylist may even open up a few seams!

What I've discovered over time is that fashion stylists know lots of excellent little tricks, especially for clothing emergencies. For instance, they know that when your hem comes undone and you don't have time to take a needle and thread to it, you should use double-sided tape to keep it in place. This was helpful for me to discover, because for years I'd just resorted to a stapler out of desperation. Other tricks they keep up their sleeve:

- If you get a stain on your clothing and don't have any packets of those great little Shout pads, see if you can get your hands on a baby wipe. They work really well on many stains.

- If you end up with deodorant marks on a dark dress or top, do not try to rub them off with your hand or a paper towel. That can make matters worse. Instead rub the mark with *another* dark piece of fabric. This is a tip I learned from our senior fashion editor Brooke Elder, who styles many of our fashion shoots, and it works quite brilliantly.

- When packing your clothes for a trip, roll your jeans and tops to prevent them from wrinkling. Items that can't be rolled should be wrapped in tissue paper.

- If your clothes do get wrinkled, try using a spray product called Downy wrinkle releaser spray (it's available online). Pack it in your bag when you travel.

- Another great way to deal with wrinkles is with a travel steamer, which costs practically nothing. It's not only good for traveling but for zapping wrinkles *anytime* because it won't leave shiny imprints like an iron often does.

- If you invested in a leather handbag that now is all scuffed up and sad, just bring it to a shoe repair shop and ask them to clean it. The results are often nearly miraculous.

- Speaking of shoe repair shops, before you even wear new shoes, take yours in for rubber soles and heels. This will make your shoes last longer and also keep the toes from scuffing. It's a bit pricey but worth it.

- The only way to really prevent visible panty line is to wear a thong. Some women don't like them because they're uncomfortable, but Brooke swears by Hanky Panky thongs, which have a wider than usual band for your butt, so they're quite comfortable.

- If you can't (yet) afford diamond studs but want earrings that add class to an outfit, buy a pair of thin fake gold hoops. It's hard to tell fake gold from real gold when it's just a hoop and the effect is classy. If you wear them every day, people will think they're your investment earrings.

SEVENTY

How to Get Awesome Cleavage

Cleavage is a *Cosmo* trademark, not only on our covers but also throughout the magazine. We often feature models and actresses in outfits that show off their breasts. It's been that way for the past forty years and it probably will be that way for the next forty. *Cosmo* used to be known for big boobs, but nowadays we feature women of all breast sizes on the cover, including very small. But since the cover always features a fairly low-cut top, we generally play up whatever cleavage our cover girls have. And they're always game.

Over time we've experimented with different methods of showcasing cleavage. Better than padded bras (or stuffing your bra with underwear, which one actress tried when we shot her) is using what fashion stylists call "chicken cutlets"— flesh-toned, gel-filled pouches shaped like, yes, chicken cutlets, which fit into a bra. But a couple of years ago we found something that my design director says is one of the best cleavage creators around: the NuBra. It's basically two cutlets, but they stick right on your boobs and are held together by a clasp. You can move them higher or lower on your breasts or closer together to get exactly the kind of cleavage you want. (They're sold on infomercials on late night TV; or go to www.fashion

forms.com.) We bring them to every cover shoot. Some actresses even arrive with their own!

If you are dressing to kill one night, consider a NuBra. The cups feel awfully sticky (it's a little like having two rodent glue traps attached to your chest), but the results are pretty awesome. Plus there aren't any straps!

SEVENTY-ONE

The 26 Best Tips I Learned from Beauty Editors

I've always been a little crazy about the world of beauty, and working at *Cosmo* has helped me indulge my obsession. We run many beauty pages in the magazine, and we cover all the new makeup and hair and skin care products. Admittedly, I groan when I read a silly term, like "buttne" (acne on your ass), coined by someone in the beauty industry; but overall, I think beauty info is really empowering. I've enjoyed sampling products and ideas, and along the way, I've picked up a ton of tricks. I have lousy hair, for instance, as flat as a car mat, but I've learned to make it much fuller with tips from the hairstylists I've worked with. Here are the twenty-six best beauty tricks I've discovered.

1. The number one way to prevent wrinkles and keep your skin healthy is by religiously wearing sunblock. Yes, your genes play a role in how you age, but sun is the biggest culprit when it comes to lines and wrinkles (not to mention skin cancer!). Wear sunscreen constantly (SPF 30), even through winter, and make sure your foundation has SPF (though you should wear sunscreen at the same time). If you want a tan, make it a fake one. There are really good fake-tanning products on the market. Exfoliate your skin

first for the best results and apply with latex gloves while you're totally naked.

2. To make your eyelashes thicker, dust them with powder before you apply mascara.

3. To shrink under-eye bags, dab on a little Preparation H— the active ingredient in it causes the blood vessels to constrict and the swelling to go down. Just don't get it within a half an inch of your eyes (and oh, never let your guy see the tube).

4. Lipstick or gloss with a blue tone will make your teeth look whiter.

5. Exfoliating really is worth the effort. You need to experiment with the kind that's right for you—scrubbing grains, for instance, or glycolic pads—but they all slough off dead skin cells and make your skin glow.

6. To add volume to your hair, absolutely *saturate* it (especially the roots) with volumizer. Lift pieces of hair as you go—it will help create air pockets, which add to the volume. When you blow-dry, lean over from the waist and dry hair from underneath until it's almost dry. Straighten up and finish by aiming the dryer at pieces of hair you've wrapped around a round brush.

7. Apply skin-moisturizing products within three minutes of stepping out of the shower or bath. That's when your skin is like a sponge and will soak the lotion up most effectively.

8. To banish hat hair, rub your locks with one of the fabric softener sheets you toss in a clothes dryer.

9. To totally dry up a zit, use Sonya Dakar Drying Potion. It works so fast that, if you apply it before bed, the pimple will be missing in action by morning. Granted, the skin in

the spot becomes a little flaky from being zapped, but who *cares*? It's better than having a zit the size of a handbag on your face.

10. To cover up a zit while you're drying it or to cover up the red area where a zit used to live, dab on a tiny bit of moisturizer first. That will help the flaky parts be less noticeable. Then apply concealer, which should be the *same shade* as your foundation (not a shade lighter, which is the right choice for under-eye bags). And the best trick of all: apply the concealer with a tiny, stiff makeup brush. This not only helps the concealer to adhere but allows you to cover the smallest area.

11. If you're going out straight from work, running damp hands through your hair will help reactivate any product you applied that morning.

12. To make bare legs gleam in summer, smooth body oil on them rather than lotion.

13. Navy mascara makes the whites of your eyes seem whiter and your eyes look less tired. You can apply it over black if you really want to darken your lashes first.

14. If it's the end of the day and you want to add more volume to dry hair, flip your hair over and mist the layers underneath with hair spray. Then shake out your hair.

15. There are wonderful skin care products out there today that really do stimulate collagen production, fight wrinkles, and slow down aging. Even if you don't have any major skin issues, make an appointment with a dermatologist and develop your own personal game plan.

16. To make your eyes look bigger, line the lower lid with a

pencil in a shade that's just a little bit lighter than the one you use for the upper lid.

17. If you feel your nose is too wide, put a little highlight cream in a line right down the center.

18. If you accidentally end up with too much product in your hair, there are rescue techniques, depending on the type of product. I learned these from Kim Serratore, who always styles my hair for CBS's *The Early Show*. If you've gone overboard with mousse, gel, or spray-on styler, brush the hell out of your hair. Because these products are alcohol-based (and are therefore dry), they'll brush out. Got the greasies from too much shine serum or smoothing cream? Sprinkle on a bit of talcum powder to absorb it. Then finger style your hair (brushing will activate the grease). And if you've OD'd on pomade or wax, blast on hairspray to help dry out the goop. Separate sticky parts with a comb.

19. Epsom salts is still one of the best things to soak in. It really does soothe achy muscles. To make the bathwater smell nice, just add a few drops of essential oil in one of your favorite fragrances.

20. My beauty director, Rachel Hayes Gayle, taught me that if you have a headful of split ends and you don't have time for a trim, you should apply some shine serum to damp ends. Then blow-dry with the nozzle pointed down so you won't cause the ends to frizz up. When your hair is dry, blast the ends with a few shots of cool air to seal them.

21. To guarantee that your makeup lasts all day, follow these steps: Put concealer or eye shadow primer on your lids first so that the shadow stays put. Use a stain on your lips and cheeks before applying lipstick and blush. After applying

makeup, dust on a light layer of powder over your whole face. Do this to your lips, too, and then reapply color and add gloss. And try not to touch your face afterwards.

22. Bronzer is a great way to fake a tan, but it can *look* fake. A great trick is to try a light coat of bronzer cream all over and then add bronzing powder to just cheeks and forehead.

23. Generally you don't need as big a quantity of a beauty product as you think. For shampoo, use a portion the size of a nickel; for night cream, the size of an M&M; for face cleanser, the size of an almond. One exception: hair volumizer. As I said before, use a ton.

24. To make your lips appear bigger, line the middle third of your upper lip (the cupid's bow) with a lip liner in the same shade as your lipstick or, even better, a highlighting pencil. Line the outer corners of your mouth with your lip liner (or use a nude liner if the colored liner is too much). Also line the center of your lower lip. Fill in with lipstick. Now add a dab of gloss right on the center of your lips.

25. Stress affects your looks—it causes your skin to break out, for instance, and makes your hair dull. Create relaxing rituals for yourself that you can always do in the evening and on weekends.

26. Last but not least, have your brows professionally groomed. So many women who attempt this job on their own bungle it, making their brows look like commas or worse, *sperm*. If you don't have someone good in your area, buy a book that shows you how to do it. Beautifully shaped eyebrows can completely transform your face.

SEVENTY-TWO

Discover the Thrill of No Panty Hose

One of the things you quickly discover when you work at a fashion magazine is that fashion editors never ever wear panty hose. I was vaguely aware of this over the years, but I didn't really zero in on it until I arrived at *Cosmo* and had a fairly large fashion department reporting to me.

The dress code in the magazine business has always been pretty loose, and all through spring and summer women in editorial keep their legs bare and wear sandals or even flip-flops. Fashion editors, however, don't limit bare legs to warm weather. As summer turned to fall my first year at *Cosmo*, I saw that the fashion department wasn't going to let the temperature drop stand in their way. They continued to bare their legs no matter how blustery the autumn winds were.

Once winter came, they opted for *some* protection. When they wore dresses or skirts, they'd pair them with boots—but with naked knees poking out at the top. Once in a blue moon you'd see one of them in black tights. And by the first of April they were right back to bare legs. It didn't matter to them, by the way, that their legs weren't the least bit tan yet. It was as if *anything* was better than stockings!

Up until that point in my life, I'd pretty much restricted myself to a sans-hose existence between Memorial Day and Labor Day. I loved going bare, experiencing the delicious sensation of naked limbs, but the idea of doing it any other time of the year seemed silly. Wouldn't it look strange? Or unprofessional? Wouldn't my legs get cold? But after a year of watching the fashion girls, I just had to try it. I figured, what was the worst that could happen—small amount of discomfort and minor windburn?

So that April, when there was still a nip in the air, I took the plunge. I wore a skirt, sling-backs, and no hose. I noticed, stepping out onto the sidewalk in front of my home in Manhattan, that my legs were brilliantly white, so white, in fact, that they were in danger of causing snow blindness in anyone passing by. And yet the color suddenly seemed better to me than the fake suntan-y or pale flesh tones of most panty hose. Besides, the feeling was *fantastic*. My legs quickly grew accustomed to the temperature and I reveled in having the sausage casing gone. For the rest of spring, I declined the hot, tight, itchy discomfort of hose.

And so I became a convert. Not in winter. I hate the cold too much. But all through the spring, summer, and fall, I have liberated limbs. And I really believe that I perform my best on those days. This may sound a little crazy, but when my legs feel unencumbered, my mind does, too.

If you're in a job where you think you need to wear hose even in summer, peel them off on a brutally hot July day and see if anyone really notices or cares. Use a little self-tanner or bronzer on them if you want color, and you can make them gleam by using a light body oil instead of lotion (my fashion director loves Nivea Silky Shimmer Lotion). If you traditionally forgo hose in summer but automatically pull them on once Labor Day arrives, try going bare instead—for as long as you can take it. Once you've discovered how good it feels, there will be no going back.

SEVENTY-THREE

The Eye Makeup Technique
That Will Make Him Gaga

I've heard people say that women wear makeup for other women, and to some extent that may be true. We want to walk into a party or an event or even into work and have other females decide that we look damn *good*. I also think we wear makeup for ourselves, for the sheer joy and pleasure of it. When you try out a new teal eyeliner pencil or shimmery gold lip gloss, it's really fun.

Plenty of times, though, we apply makeup with men in mind—because we want to snag one, seduce one, enchant one, reinforce the decision of one who has already chosen us, or make one who has ditched us eat his bloody heart out. So in those instances the question becomes, what kind of makeup do *men* really dig? If you are clearly on a man mission, what should you go for?

Well, it depends a little bit on the man. But I feel safe making some broad statements based on what I've learned.

1. Guys hate too much makeup, especially foundation that makes your skin look like the shade of a Band-Aid and anything goopy on your lips that suggests they will become stuck to your mouth if they attempt to kiss you.

2. They also hate too *little* makeup. Despite how much they rave about the natural look, most guys want you to make a fuss with your appearance. It shows you care.

3. And if there is one makeup effect they really go bonkers over, it's what makeup artists call smoky eyes—eyes that are lined with black and covered with deep gray shadow.

Why do smoky eyes fire up guys? I think it's in large part because they're so mysterious. Helen Fisher, research professor and member of the Center for Evolutionary Studies in the Department of Anthropology at Rutgers University, says that we humans are programmed to mate outside of the family group and thus it's the unfamiliar and the mysterious that really turns us on. Also, distinctive eye makeup draws attention to the eyes, which, according to Fisher, are the only feature that actually gives insight into what's going on in the brain.

To create a smoky eye, first apply concealer or an eye shadow primer so the color will stay put and not get blotchy. Rim the area along your upper lashes with a black pencil that you've sharpened the heck out of so it doesn't go on too thickly. Start from the inner eye and work outward, pulling each lid tautly as you work so that you can come as close to the lashes—even *into* the lashes—as possible. Now line the lower lid, too. Then smudge the liner ever so gently with your fingertips. This will prevent the line from appearing harsh and also create a "bedroom eye" feel. Next apply a charcoal or deep gray shadow to your lids, going just slightly above the crease (otherwise you'll risk looking like a raccoon). You may have to experiment with eye shadows because some grays can smear and look messy. For an extra special touch, you can add a pearlized gray highlighting shadow to the area along your brow bone. Finish by curling your lashes and applying very black mascara.

The rest of your face needs to be nicely balanced so you don't look Goth. Pick a soft color for your cheeks and then try a matte lipstick or gloss in nude or a brownish pink. For the right occasion, red lips can look pretty dramatic with smoky eyes, but for a basic date or party, that effect is probably going to be too overpowering. Keep your lips more neutral.

Now, you are ready to enchant.

SEVENTY-FOUR

How to Look as Sexy as J.Lo

Have you ever noticed how Jennifer Lopez looks sexy in practically every single shot you see of her? I was discussing this with my deputy entertainment editor the day before she interviewed the actress/singer/style icon for her third *Cosmo* cover.

"It's not just because of her face and her hair and clothes," I said. "There's something so hot and sultry about her expression. She's the embodiment of sexiness."

The day after the interview, the editor stopped me in the hall.

"I've got something for you," she said. "From my J.Lo interview."

No, it wasn't a signed CD. It was the secret to the sexiness factor. Jennifer Lopez told my editor that the trick to looking really sexy in a picture is to have a very sexy thought in your head the moment the photo is being taken.

And part of the fun is that no one gets to know what it is!

SEVENTY-FIVE

How to Add Instant Magic to a Room

I love to entertain in my home, but I'm not naturally clever at creating fabulous table settings or magical ambiance. Because of that I'm always looking for little tricks I can *steal*—as long as they don't require real skill or a hot glue gun.

In chapter 11 I mentioned that I'd had the opportunity to get to know Colin Cowie, the event planner extraordinaire, and so whenever I'm in a room with him, I try to lap up *everything* he says. Though Colin spares no expense when he's putting on his events, some of his wonderful ideas are actually easy and cheap to replicate.

When he was helping to plan *Cosmo*'s fortieth birthday bash, the discussion eventually worked its way to lighting. Colin planned to create awesome effects with artificial light but also with candles. At one point he announced dramatically, "There's no such thing as too many votive candles."

As soon as he said that, I flashed back to a party I'd been to the year before at Marlo Thomas's apartment. I don't know her personally but she'd hosted an event one night to stimulate interest in a good cause, and I ended up on the guest list.

Her place was really awesome. Though it was on the Upper East Side, facing Central Park, it had a bit of a downtown loft feeling—with a big open space that seemed to be living room, dining room, and library in one. There was a breathtaking view of the park and the West Side beyond it, sparkling with lights. It was such a kick to be in the apartment of "That Girl," and also to find it so amazing. Midway through the party, as I was leaving the powder room, I discovered her husband, Phil Donahue, herding several women down a hallway. He'd obviously discovered them snooping around the expansive back part of the apartment. The guests looked pretty sheepish but I couldn't blame them. I would have killed for a full tour.

And yet as dazzling as the apartment and view were that night, what had struck me the most (and this is what I remembered when Colin made his comment) were the many candles on every surface. They twinkled enchantingly and made the space seem absolutely magical. Some were scented and smelled very exotic.

I'd drifted away from using votive candles over the years, but after hearing Colin's proclamation, I started plopping them all around when I entertained. If you are in a huge hurry or don't want to spend a bundle, they are a simple way to make a room glamorous, mysterious, and seductive.

PART SIX

YOU ON TOP

Life

SEVENTY-SIX

Start Strong

ast fall, on the first day of New York Fashion Week, my fashion director, Michelle McCool, mentioned a funny exchange she'd overheard at one of the shows between an editor in chief of a magazine and an underling. The woman gushed to the editor about how stunning she looked in the designer dress she was wearing that day. "Thanks," the editor replied. "I've *always* believed that the key to Fashion Week is starting strong."

I could see why the woman on my staff found it so amusing. The editor had spoken as if she were in some kind of horse race—and you could just imagine the words of the announcer. "And they're off. Editor X sprints into the early lead in a forty-five-hundred-dollar Dolce and Gabbana dress."

And yet even though that editor's comment seemed so silly and self-important, I knew there was a kernel of wisdom embedded in it—not necessarily in relation to dressing but in terms of going after things that you want in work and in life. It *is* smart to start strong. To grab something good while you can. To be unafraid to make a big bang in the beginning.

I didn't always buy into that philosophy. I'd heard people talk about the importance of keeping something in reserve and of *finishing* strong, especially in certain sports. I remember hearing a tennis commentator at the U.S. Open say that if you were one of the top players, you knew to save your best tennis for the second week. Pacing yourself mattered, I thought, and I practiced it in work situations, occasionally hoarding the best so that I could use it at just the right moment. But over time I came to see the merit in *not* holding too much good stuff in reserve. I learned the advantage of putting a dazzling idea or two out there right away.

Because if you start strong, you create a halo effect: people remember the first thing, often regardless of what comes after. Besides, things change, and certain opportunities to dazzle may not present themselves again.

This really crystallized for me when I went with my entertainment editor to meet with Faith Hill's publicist about doing a *Cosmo* cover. It was the late nineties and I thought Faith would make a perfect cover. Her music was hugely popular, she had many *Cosmo* readers among her fans, and though she was married with a couple of kids, she looked sexy as anything. I figured that her publicist would instantly recognize what a terrific fit it would be.

But unfortunately he didn't see it that way at all. He told us that he was concentrating on securing her covers on some of the women's service magazines (*McCall's* was one of the first he worked out), and he could always do *Cosmo* later. We tried to politely impress on him what we saw as our advantage: we sold far more copies on the newsstand than any of the women's service magazines. Plus, those magazines were for older women and we offered the perfect opportunity for Faith to connect with younger fans while she was still pretty young herself. But we couldn't sway him. We left the building shaking our heads in dismay.

Fast-forward to a couple of years later. We received a call out of the blue offering us a cover of Faith to tie in with her new CD. But it was too late. By then she had *three* kids and she'd been on all those women's service magazines. Her image now seemed too soccer mom for *Cosmo*.

Granted, celebrities do need careful PR strategies or they become overexposed or tainted from doing the wrong kind of publicity. But that publicist's decision always seemed dumb to me. Why not score a *Cosmo* cover when you had the chance? Because the offer might not come around again.

So don't hold back. If you've got a great idea, blow their minds with it *now* instead of delaying until all your ducks are in a perfect row. If you've bought a killer outfit for your new job, go ahead and wear it the first day (as long as you're sure it makes sense for your new workplace). If someone presents you with an amazing opportunity, grab it now, rather than waiting for just the right moment.

SEVENTY-SEVEN

Think Like a Bitch but Talk as Sweet as Bambi

There's no question that if you need to make a situation go your way, acting like a bitch can sometimes be the ticket. People often become intimidated when you start shouting or braying at them. As a result, they may snap-to and do your bidding.

There's also a certain satisfaction, even exhilaration, that comes from expressing the authentic annoyance and anger you're experiencing at a given moment (particularly if you have a habit of sucking it up like a good girl). Not long ago, a friend of mine told me that she'd been having problems with a guy in another department at work. She occasionally has to collaborate on projects with him, and to put it mildly, the guy can be a real prick. On one of their recent tasks, he signed off on a major component without telling her, and she was so mad that she stormed over to his office for a showdown. He wasn't there but his secretary was.

"Please say I dropped by," she told the woman. "And let him know that there was smoke coming out of my ass."

As she walked back to her office, she said she was positively giddy from having said exactly what she felt rather than squashing it like she typically does.

But there's a problem with bitchiness. It may feel good at the moment, just like devouring a bucket of butter-flavored movie pop-corn, but there are often negative reverberations later. Also, bitch-iness doesn't always get you what you want.

I think that's partly due to the fact that being a bitch has lost the element of surprise it once had. Ten or fifteen years ago bitches were fewer in number. They made up this kind of elite squad, and so when you encountered one, it could have a pow-erful impact. But today they're everywhere you are. Cheryl Del-lasega, Ph.D., the author of *Mean Girls Grown Up* and a professor at Penn, told us that women have gotten bitchier in re-cent years and says it's a result of the sense of entitlement we feel. "Women go all out for what they want today," she says. "That's good, except this increasingly competitive environment has meant that women can be more focused on outwitting each other."

With so many bitches out there, people are often inured to their behavior—and *don't* snap-to. Plus, in many instances the person being bitched out knows that despite the threats being hurled at her, there won't actually be any negative consequences. For instance, you can tell the rude airline clerk that you'll have her job, but she knows that's *soooo* not gonna happen. In many in-stances the only reaction you're going to trigger by behaving like a bitch is to have someone roll their eyes or sneer at you.

Even when bitchiness produces results to your liking, it can backfire later. I've seen it cause lots of nasty ripple effects—what you might call the bitch chain reaction. The person you've of-fended may malign you later to others, fail to pass on critical info to you, not do something when they're supposed to, or even rant about you in a blog. Or your behavior may just plain discom-bobulate people in a way that ends up biting *you* in the butt. A couple of years ago I jumped into a taxi with a business colleague who has a bit of a bitchy streak. We'd no sooner closed the door than she was asking the driver to turn down the a.c. He fiddled with the knob and then shifted his concentration back to the bumper-to-bumper traffic on Sixth Avenue. We'd traveled less than a minute when she barked at him, "Driver, I *asked* you to turn down the a.c." Nervously he reached for the knob again— and we promptly rammed into the car in front of us. Sure, the car felt less like a deep freeze, but we then had to wait ten minutes while the drivers exchanged info.

One interesting phenomenon I see these days is *selective* bitchiness—or in other words, picking and choosing whom to lose it with. Some celebs are especially guilty of this. If you're an underling on their movie set, you may not be allowed to make eye contact with them, but if you're a reporter interviewing them for a story, they turn on the charm full blast. I'm convinced that they think that the world-at-large won't learn about their nasty doings. But the truth just leaks out sooner or later. When we shoot a *Cosmo* cover, most actresses we work with are great and some— like Beyoncé, Kate Hudson, and Molly Sims—couldn't be dreamier. Occasionally, however, we'll run into a star who just isn't that easy to deal with. And the funny thing is, it *always* shows up later in the photos. We did a cover once on an A-list actress who is legendary for being "a real sweetheart" to her co-stars, but she can be brutal to deal with in other situations. On our shoot, the hairstylist—whom she'd picked herself—offered to trim her hair a little bit, which seemed like a really stupid thing to do right before a big photo session. Sure enough, the actress looked down at one point, saw that the pile of hair was bigger than she'd expected, and threw a total hissy fit, claiming that it was a conspiracy on *our* part to make certain her hair was shorter for the photo. (I guess she hadn't noticed that we like lots of hair on our covers.) She threatened to walk off the set that second. The team was able to calm her down but she remained in a bad mood—until, of course, she posed for her pictures. Then she gave us her sweetheart side. But here's the funny part. Her bitchy mood managed to come through in every single frame and our only choice was to go with the least offensive one. When you look at her face on that cover, it seems as if she's thinking, "My latest movie just tanked, my boyfriend just dumped me, and my underwear is currently wedged in my butt crack." It was one of the worst selling covers since I've been at *Cosmo*.

Okay, so if bitchiness doesn't work, what does? Well, I've learned that it's okay to *think* like a bitch—to feel annoyed or frustrated by what someone's trying to pull—but when it comes to taking action, it's better to resort to sugar lips, like little Bambi. Be nice, be patient, be attentive. I don't always manage to follow this approach but when I do, it works unbelievably well. The next time you are in a situation that makes you want to fly off the handle (*or* someone is being bitchy to you), try the following:

- Take a deep breath (through your nose so they won't notice) and silently count to five. Yes, it calms you down, but it also has an interesting effect on the other person. It allows them to catch their breath and it makes them curious about where you're headed.
- Ask questions that will clarify the situation for you. This not only prevents you from getting all riled up for no reason (the plane *has* been canceled but the good news is that they are putting you on another flight leaving in twenty-five minutes),

it also enables you to calm down even more and think through the situation.

- Once you have all the info, convey to the other person that you understand whatever predicament he or she is in. Harried airline clerks, waiters, receptionists, and flight attendants are just a few of the types who appreciate this, because people rarely see it from their side. Then explain your own situation as quickly as possible, summing up what you'd like to have happen so that information doesn't get lost. End by—and this part is important—*empowering* the person to help you. For instance, let's say you've just arrived at a restaurant with a friend and you've been told by the maître d' that he has no record of your reservation. Say something like "I realize you're very busy right now, but I would really appreciate your help. I know I have a reservation because I made it myself. Perhaps the person who took it down put it on the wrong day. I promised my friend to take her here and it would mean so much to me if you could work something out for us."

  Granted, it will irk you to have to suck up your frustration like this, and it doesn't *always* work. But I think your chances are better with this approach than with "the bitch stomp." I spoke with a waiter recently who revealed that when rude people request variations on a dish, he and the other servers say that the kitchen can't do it—without even checking. But nice diners are rarely turned down.

- If you have a chip you can play (like your father is a friend of the owner or you are a regular customer), go ahead but don't lord it over the person. I find that saying something like, "I've recommended your restaurant so many times, and I'm very *disappointed* with what's happening," has a lot of impact. People seem to respond to the D word.

Even if someone is being bitchy to you first, it still helps to acknowledge the other person's needs. We once did an evening shoot with a celebrity—not an actress, but someone in the news—and just before she went to sign the photo release form, she caught sight of herself in a mirror and decided not to sign. Apparently she had drunk a fair amount of wine during the shoot and she now thought she looked, in her words, "like I've just been fucked." Without the release, we couldn't run the photos.

I'd just heard of the crisis the next morning when my assistant announced that the woman was on the phone. As soon as I said hello, she went off on a tear about how horrible she'd looked and that she just couldn't authorize use of the photos. What I was tempted to say was, "The next time you do a photo shoot, stay away from the pinot grigio." But instead I told her, "This must be very upsetting for you. Let me order the film right away and take a look. And then we can figure out what we can do."

After I saw the photos, I called her back and told her I agreed, that in some of the later pictures her hair and makeup did look a little sloppy. But I said that the ones from earlier in the evening were lovely and I thought she'd be happy with those. I sent her over a sample—not for approval but just for her to see—and she told me she was happy with the choice and also very grateful. "The minute you told me you could understand what I was talking about, I was so relieved," she said.

That's really the essence of the Bambi approach and why it works so much better than bitching. People are anxious for you to *get* them, and they tend to respond well when you do.

Besides, with the Bambi approach you also have the element of surprise on your side, something the bitchy approach no longer offers.

SEVENTY-EIGHT

Every Woman Adores
a Bag of Beauty Loot

In the *Cosmo* offices there is a little room that is so special and enticing that we have to keep it securely locked at all times. Only I and one other person have a key. Can you guess what it is? No, it's not the room where we store all the sex manuals we use for research. *It's the beauty closet.*

All magazines that run beauty stories have some type of beauty closet. It's where editors keep the hair and skin care products and makeup that get sent to the magazine for coverage. We feature twenty beauty pages a month in *Cosmo* and therefore have an especially jam-packed beauty closet.

Several times a year our beauty editors need to clean out the closet to make room for newer stuff, and they have a beauty giveaway for the staff, or what you might call a bull-shark feeding frenzy because staffers who attend go totally crazy. We all rummage through big cartons of lip glosses and moisturizers and hairstyling products and fill bags with whatever our hearts desire—though it's sometimes necessary to stick an elbow in the ribs of a co-worker or two. When my kids were little and I brought them into work, they would just love to visit the beauty closet to snag a few products. My son even asked me once, "Mom, can we go to beauty today?"

Part of the allure of the beauty closet is that you're getting something for free. Who doesn't love a freebie? But I think it's also *what* you're getting for free. Some of the products in the closet are basics like shampoo and shower gel, but many are luxurious items you wouldn't necessarily buy for yourself. Honestly, how often do you treat yourself to a tub of body butter smelling of green tea or a tube of luscious Chanel lipstick? So being able to just scarf them up is absolutely delightful. It's the same reason people love the swag bags of goodies given out at star-studded events in L.A. and New York.

Realizing what a kick I, my staff, and my kids got from the loot in the beauty closet, I started giving out beauty bags to women in certain situations—for instance, to a writer who dropped by the office or a business associate I was meeting. They seemed to go nuts for these little bags. Once I had to escort the head of a movie studio to an awards ceremony, and I prepared a big beauty bag for her, leaving it at her hotel the night before. Someone who saw what I was doing suggested that this was a silly gesture considering that the woman I was escorting was amazingly rich and successful, but the next day the studio head told me she spent an hour going through the bag before she went to bed!

A couple of times I've even let someone visit the beauty closet and pick out products herself—like a version of those supermarket shopping sprees. Each woman who did it seemed perfectly giddy during the experience. But after one particular incident I had to bring the practice to a halt. I'd asked a reality TV star I'd met to come by the office and talk at one of our *Cosmo* salons, and in return for the favor I told her she could fill a bag with items from the beauty closet. After her talk, she headed down to the closet with her publicist and the associate beauty editor. Later the editor called me in a tizzy to report that our beauty closet had been completely denuded. "She was there for an hour," the editor told me, "and I didn't know how to stop her. She filled up bags and bags. And she didn't take just makeup and skin stuff; she took everything that wasn't nailed down—a hair dryer, deodorant, toothpaste. The funny thing is, the whole time she was complaining about how hard it was being famous."

Okay, so now I'm back to doing the bags myself. But that doesn't change the underlying principle. If you want to make a woman feel positively gleeful—because it's her birthday or she's been in the dumps or she's pissed at you because you spend all your time with your new boyfriend and haven't called her in two weeks—line a little bag with colored tissue paper and fill it with a few special beauty products and give it to her. Just be sure to include a tub of body butter!

SEVENTY-NINE

How to Find the Time to Do the Things You Really, Really Want

Despite how thrilling it was to land the *Cosmo* job, there was one aspect of it that broke my heart. About half a year before I was offered the position, I'd begun writing my first murder mystery, and as I was accepting the job, one of the thoughts flashing through my brain like a security alarm was, *Oh damn, there goes the mystery.* I knew I would have to abandon it.

In my previous position—as editor of *Redbook*—writing a book on the side hadn't posed a problem. I had my job pretty much under control and I only had to lug work home a couple of nights a week. I was able to snatch time here and there to work on my mystery, and I loved it. I had developed a soupçon of career malaise, and I found that imagining corpses and killers was shaking me out of my slump.

But *Cosmo* was a much bigger fish to fry than *Redbook*, and I knew I would be a fool not to give it my undivided attention from the start. I could just imagine what my boss would have said if I announced during our interview that I also planned to write a mystery that year. She would have probably murdered *me*.

During my first months at *Cosmo*, I would occasionally think of my gutsy, irreverent, amateur sleuth, Bailey Weggins, and feel a twinge of sadness as I pictured her stuck in a drawer, cooling her heels. I was thrilled with my new opportunity but I hated sidelining Bailey.

Why did I have such a big yearning to write a mystery? Partly because the fabulous, fearless Nancy Drew was one of my first role models and she inspired me to want to create my own detective. Plus, I'm in such a precarious business that I've always liked the notion of having a Plan B in case I am given the boot. While plotting out how I was going to shape *Cosmo*'s future and picking out sexy bustiers for the cover, I promised myself that someday I'd find my way back to Bailey Weggins.

Then a funny thing happened. It was Christmastime, about six months after I started, and since I had a few vacation days, I decided to drag my four chapters out of the drawer. As I reread what I'd written, I discovered that I'd had Bailey find the dead nanny sprawled on a copy of *Cosmo*, something I'd completely forgotten doing. I couldn't even recall *Cosmo* being much on my radar back then. So you know what? I took it as a clear sign that I was meant to combine editing *Cosmo* and writing mysteries. Since that day I have published four Bailey Weggins murder mysteries: *If Looks Could Kill*, *A Body to Die For*, *'Til Death Do Us Part*, and *Over Her Dead Body*.

The challenge, of course, was figuring out how to accomplish both without doing a lousy job at either one. In fact, the question I get asked most when I give a speech or an interview is, "How do you *do* it?" I know why that question is so popular. Most of us who dream of writing a book, starting a jewelry line, or creating awe-inspiring sculptures can't afford to leave our jobs (at least initially), and so we're desperate for any advice on how to juggle successfully. For me, mystery writing hasn't exactly been a breeze, but it's been *doable* and that's because of two little strategies I've relied on. Here's what they are. If you try them, I swear they'll work for you, too.

Strategy 1: To find the time, you must *make* the time.

It sounds obvious but in order to tackle a major goal—whether it's writing your first novel or *finally* putting all the pictures in your photo albums—you have to block out the time to do it and view that time as sacred. It's easy to believe that if you feel passionate enough about something, the time for it will magically present itself during the course of the day. But that doesn't just happen. You must designate a certain period when you're going to do the job—and you may have to experiment a bit to figure out what works best for you. Despite the fact that I had written two nonfiction books in the evening (with one eye on *Law and Order* or *ER* most of the time), I realized that fiction came most easily to me in the mornings. So after trial and error, I began blocking off time on weekends when my kids were sleeping (they're teenagers so they don't raise a head off the pillow until at least eleven) and on weekdays before my staff arrived.

Once you designate a block of time for a goal, you will probably wonder how you're supposed to do what *used* to happen in that time period. Interestingly, when you organize your time, you become more efficient at accomplishing your to-do list. You putter less, end phone calls earlier, etc., and what you used to do in that slot probably will gravitate to your "found time." But if your schedule is impossibly packed and you're already an efficient machine, it may not be possible to shoehorn a project into your life without letting something else go. Then you have to throw a few things overboard. In order to write my mysteries, I gave up tennis (I was pathetic anyway), leisurely shopping excursions (I do miss that), and sleeping late on Saturday and Sunday mornings (miss that, too!). But for me, the trade-off was worth it.

Strategy 2: To actually be productive in your time slot, you have to learn to *slice the salami.*

As we all know, just because you block off time doesn't mean you will accomplish anything constructive in it. I was a pro at telling myself that I would write in the morning and then *not doing it.* That's because writing often seemed so tough. I dreaded the notion of sitting there for hours trying to put words to computer.

I was saved by a technique called "slice the salami." When I was a young writer, I interviewed a time management expert named Edwin Bliss (one of his books is called *Getting It Done*) who had devised this particular approach. His point was that if you make a project too big, it seems like a huge hunk of salami. Now, there's nothing very appetizing about *that.* But if you carve it into thin slices, it's much more appealing.

Bliss says we have to do this with projects, too—in other words, slice them down into appealing pieces. For instance, don't promise yourself you're going to put your entire photo album together on Saturday. Just say that you are going to spend one hour getting started by sorting as many photos as possible by *date.*

You'll have to figure out for yourself how thin your slices need to be in order to seem manageable for you. I knew, because I'd always tended to put off writing, that mine had to be very, very skinny. So for the first few months, I told myself I would only write for fifteen minutes a day.

Well, fifteen minutes turned out to be the secret for me. And something interesting happened. After fifteen minutes, I'd usually keep at it, because I had a nice flow going. Eventually I extended my salami slice. It's up to two hours now (and I also discovered that it helped to aim for a certain number of *pages* during that period). But I know that it's smart not to take it beyond that or I just won't want to dig in. I frequently write for *four* hours, but if I set myself a goal of four hours, I'd never sit down at my desk.

Admittedly it's been nutty at times to do *two* jobs. But overall it's been a good thing. The book writing has given my brain a chance to refuel for *Cosmo*, and working at *Cosmo* has given me killer ideas for my books.

EIGHTY

How to Keep a Secret

K eeping a secret can be a bitch. When you acquire a delicious piece of gossip or news, you almost can't help but feel the urge to blab, even if you have been begged not to.

It doesn't take long for people to recognize whether you're the type who guards a confidence or can't keep her trap shut. And once they figure you out, they treat you accordingly. Good things tend to come to secret keepers. They become privy to other confidences. They are given information that can prove useful—as long as they are discreet. They may be allowed entrée to an inner sanctum.

I'm a good secret keeper. Not because I'm such an amazingly upright person. Hey, my first instinct is to *want* to tell. But I learned a neat trick years ago for keeping info under wraps. The reason I trained myself is that back in my twenties I divulged a tidbit I should have kept under wraps. Though I take full responsibility, I should point out that the information was extracted by a woman who could sneak a bone away from a pit bull. I vowed after my infraction that I was going to learn to zip my lips, and my track record today is excellent. In fact, for several years I've known a secret that is so huge that it would make headlines, but I have never breathed a word of it to anyone because the person who told me asked me not to.

Here's the trick. Instead of viewing a secret as something you need to unload, think of it as something so good it must be *hoarded*. Allow yourself to savor it and appreciate having it all to yourself. Let a smile cross your face when you are thinking about it. If you really relish a piece of information, and consider how important you feel possessing it when practically no one else does, you won't want to give it away.

EIGHTY-ONE

Dumb *Little* Decisions Often Lead to Dumb *Big* Decisions (So Don't Make the Little Ones)

Have you ever said yes to having a drink with a guy not because you wanted to spend even one hour in his company but because it just seemed easier to acquiesce rather than go through all the clunkiness of turning him down? You told yourself you'd manage to survive one drink, and besides, you'd have a friend call you on your cell while you were in the bar and make it seem like there was a crisis that necessitated your leaving early.

The problem with this kind of strategy—as you may have learned—is that as soon as you snap your cell phone closed and announce to this guy whom you never plan to see again (no, nothing changed during drinks) that you have to leave *this second* because your friend's cat was just diagnosed with a terminal tumor and your friend is a blubbering wreck, he asks if you'd like to get together for dinner Saturday night.

Now you're suddenly faced with another decision and it's even trickier than the previous one. Last time you were just talking to this dude on the phone, but now you're face to face, which makes things even more awkward. Plus, a whole host of excuses you could have used before ("I have a boyfriend"; "My Teach for

America gig starts next week") will no longer have the same ring of authenticity because you've accepted the drink. You may even say yes to the dinner and then tell yourself you will wiggle out of that later.

We've all been there—found ourselves in an avoidable jam because we earlier said yes to something we didn't have to.

I've gotten good about not making dumb little decisions, because at *Cosmo* there's too big of a price to pay if they later lead you into making dumb *big* ones. I'd rather be ruthless upfront, even if it's tough or awkward, and thus avoid even bigger problems down the line.

Here's a decent example, though I wince when I remember it. About a year after I arrived, we sent a big crew of people— photographer, photographer's assistants, fashion director, design director, entertainment editor, makeup artist, hairstylist—out to L.A. to shoot a cover of a very beautiful up-and-coming Hollywood star. I thought this girl was amazing. But a few days before the shoot, we were informed that her hair was a big problemo. It had been cut very short so she could wear a wig in the movie she was filming.

Nice of them to finally tell us, right? And it made the situation especially tough for us: one of the trademarks of *Cosmo* covers is big hair, which generally means long. Short *can* work but it's gotta be full and gorgeous. We consulted with the hairstylist we were using and he said he'd pack a ton of volumizer, extensions, and even a bunch of wigs, though it was too late to order anything customized for this particular actress.

The day of the shoot I received a phone call from my design director saying that things were much worse than we'd imagined. The actress's hair was not just short, it was *really, really* short.

Jeanne d'Arc short (or at least how they show her in movies). There was no way any volume could be infused. It was also too short for extensions. And the icing on the cake? It was a kind of orangey color with dark roots. Oh, wait, there was one more thing—her hair was totally fried from all the coloring it had been subjected to.

The hairstylist had tried a few wigs but they didn't look natural. The plan, my design director said, was to style the actress's own hair as best as they could, and hope that it looked better on film than in real life.

But here was the hitch with that strategy. If her hair looked crappy in person, it would most likely look crappy on film. And no amount of retouching would help. Photoshop allows you to erase blemishes on the face and wrinkles in dresses, but it's not so good with hair—if you attempt to adjust the color in any way, the results just look smeared.

So not only would the actress have to appear on *Cosmo* with fried orange hair, but chances were that the short, short hair would give her a pinheady look. Not at all elements of a winning cover.

"Not good," I said.

"Well, let's just try and see what happens," my design director said. What she was advocating was the wise thing to do politically, but I knew at that moment that I couldn't agree to it. That's because once the film came in, I'd find myself on a terribly slippery slope. The actress's people would be *expecting* a cover because we'd shot it, and if I didn't like the film and pulled out, they would be furious. Even if the cover team wasn't wild about the final film, they might push for the cover because they had a lot invested in it. I could easily find myself appeasing everyone by going forward with a cover that I knew wouldn't sell.

So I told the group to simply pack up and come home—without taking a single photo.

It was awful. People were totally bummed out, and later I learned one person even cried. But I never regretted my choice. I made a messy decision that prevented me from a cover disaster four months later.

So the next time you find yourself about to give in to something because it's just easier to say yes, ask yourself what situations it could lead to. Make the smart choice now, even though it may be tough—and spare yourself misery later.

So what did I do for a cover that month? I went with a gorgeous blonde fashion model. And the actress? She went on to become a major star and I may never convince her to try again (though I hope to). Still, I think a cover of her in orange hair would have been a dud. The cover with the blonde model sold over two million copies on the newsstand.

EIGHTY-TWO

How to Be a Great Listener

Many women seem to be naturally good listeners. And it's a quality that serves them well, not only in their friendships and romantic relationships, but also in their work. When women first poured into the workforce in the 1970s, they were encouraged to think and act like men, but management experts today say that in the modern workplace, where there's a great value placed on emotional intelligence, abilities like listening and intuiting are helping women move up the ladder more quickly than men in some cases.

Listening is such a powerful skill that I'm always intrigued by someone who does it really well. One of the best listeners I've met through my job is Dr. Keith Ablow, MD, the forensic psychiatrist, novelist, and author of *Inside the Mind of Scott Peterson*. I met with him to discuss a piece for *Cosmo* on how to recognize a dangerous man. Talking to him is intoxicating. He seems genuinely fascinated about what you are saying, and curious to know more. At several points during our breakfast, I was afraid I was going to blurt out every secret in my life—and perhaps even confess to a few crimes I'd never committed.

To be a good listener, Dr. Ablow says that it's important to train yourself to be quiet. Really hear the other person's words and don't automatically rush in with your own story. You almost need to be somewhat removed from the conversation and become an observer of yourself as a listener.

And pay attention to what you might call the "pebbles" in their words, anything that's slightly improbable or incongruous. Stay with those and then ask about them. Dr. Ablow says that once when he met a stripper, he asked her why she did what she did. She told him, "I don't know—the first time I tried it, it just felt like home." He then asked, "What was home like?" And she burst into tears.

One more point. Ablow says that one technique psychiatrists use to help a person open up is to rephrase what he or she has said in the form of a question or statement. For instance, a friend says to you, "I never visit my parents, anymore; it's just too crazy." You say, "It sounds like it's really important for you to distance yourself from that craziness."

When you reiterate the response, says Ablow, "the person will often tell you more of his truth. People are looking for an invitation. They don't want to be strangers."

EIGHTY-THREE

3 Ways to Stay Safe
and Outsmart Danger

O kay, admittedly this chapter seems a little out of place among topics like the right way to be kiss-assy and how to develop a signature sex move. But I've learned a lot about personal safety since I've been editor of *Cosmo*. That's because we cover the subject frequently in the magazine. But it's also because I write murder mysteries and I've had the opportunity to consult with many experts about crime and safety.

Some of the best advice I've heard comes from Barbara Butcher, director of forensic investigation and disaster coordination for the New York City Chief Medical Examiner's Office. Barbara began her career in the M.E.'s office by doing fieldwork—she was one of the people who go to the scene of a homicide and begin the process of determining the cause of death. She's a remarkable person and awesomely talented, and she's helped me with all my mysteries. I asked her to speak at one of our recent *Cosmo* salons because I thought my staff would find it fascinating and beneficial.

That day she talked to my staff not only about her work but also about how they could protect themselves in dangerous situations. There are three points she gave that have really stayed with me.

1. If something feels wrong, it *is*. Too often women ignore their gut instinct in a situation. We worry that we're overreacting or being paranoid and that if we take action, we'll look silly or even rude. For instance, let's say you find yourself in an underground parking garage one evening and there's only one other person, a guy lingering by his car. You find it slightly odd that he seems to be taking an extra long time to unlock his car, and your stomach tightens. But then you begin rationalizing. The guy is in a suit, so how much of a criminal could he be? Maybe you're just feeling wigged out because it's late and you're alone. But heed Barbara's advice. If it feels wrong, it is. Turn on your heels, hurry back to the ground level, and find a guard to walk you to your car or call a male friend and ask him to come meet you. Don't worry that you may seem like a scaredy-cat.

2. Scream *before* you're in trouble. Barbara says that screams really can drive a predator away, but the best time to yell is when nothing's happening yet. If you scream when he starts to attack you, he may be too caught up in his actions to stop, and your screams could even incite him to be *more* violent. But if you scream before anything transpires, he may decide it's smarter to leave you alone. Let's say you're walking down a street late at night and a guy passes you. You become aware that he's reached the corner, turned around, and is headed back in your direction. Don't wait to see if he's going to do anything. Scream now. At the top of your lungs. Because he's not fully invested in hurting you yet, you may drive him away.

3. Whenever you find yourself in a potential crisis, take a deep breath and spend a few seconds or so trying to calm yourself before you do anything. After the 2004 tsunami I read a quote from a tourist who said that as he became caught up in a stampede of people fleeing a resort, he noticed a local person make a turn and head down a passageway. He told himself that someone local might know the way better. And he was right. By following the man, the tourist quickly reached higher ground. Being able to think clearly in a crisis can be lifesaving. But to think clearly, you have to calm down and allow yourself time to process what's happening.

What Barbara says is that a deep breath and a few seconds can be enough to calm you. "Use those three seconds," she says, "to find the strong woman inside you who is going to handle the situation as intelligently and rationally as possible."

EIGHTY-FOUR

8 Ways to Get Someone to Say Yes

I believe so much in the power of asking that in my first book, *Why Good Girls Don't Get Ahead but Gutsy Girls Do*, I devoted a big chunk to the importance of doing it even if it makes you nervous as hell.

In life, the squeaky wheel really does get the grease. If you want something, you generally have to take the initiative and ask. Why, if you deserve it, should you be the one making the effort? Well, the other person may be holding out because he doesn't actually *know* you want it or simply because you're not making any fuss.

Though I'm aware that it's incredibly important to ask, I'm not naturally very good at it. So I've tried to become a student of asking. I've observed people who do it well and learned from them.

Here are some tips I've gathered in my *Cosmo* years:

1. Just do it. No matter how pathetic you are at making the pitch, doing it poorly is better than not doing it at all. Plunge ahead and just spit the words out. They will not think you are greedy or needy. They will respect you for asking, even if it's begrudgingly.

2. Think of your opening line as a little Corvette that zips down the highway, hugging the road tightly. In other words, get your request out in one shot and don't waver.

This is a technique I've seen used by the most dynamic publishers I've worked with (they're the ones who oversee the business side of the magazine including ad page sales). They don't beat around the bush and they never flinch. Probably the best way to guarantee that you do this successfully is to write down your request and rehearse it beforehand.

3. Make clear to the person you're talking to how giving you what you want is advantageous not just to you but to her as well. People like doing things for you when they benefit from the arrangement. It's just human nature. But I can't tell you how often a person makes a request of me and neglects to include this perspective. For instance, someone on my staff once asked for a bigger office with a window because, in her view, she had been on the job long enough to deserve it and not having a window made her grumpy. Trust me, I would have found her request so much more appealing if she'd said something like "I've made a long-term commitment to grow here and give you my best, and I would love my office to represent that commitment."

Another trait I've noticed in good publishers is that they listen very, very closely at meetings with clients. They pick up clues as to what a client's needs are and then try to make a sale based on satisfying those needs.

4. But at the same time that you're letting the other party know what's in it for them, don't be afraid to show how delighted you'll be—even honored—if you end up taking home the prize. Even though being on the cover of *Cosmo* is a plum, my amazing entertainment editor,

Tracy Shaffer, always lets the publicist she's pitching know how thrilled we would be to have a certain celebrity on the cover. She believes this allows the other person to enjoy that *they* are delivering something to us, rather than just the other way around.

5. Present both the pros and cons. I had the chance recently to talk to Kevin Hogan, who is a motivational speaker and the author of *The Science of Influence: How to Get Anyone to Say Yes in Eight Minutes or Less*. He believes that presenting the reason the person might *not* want to go along, as well as the reason you think he should, can often advance your case. When you say something like "I know I've only been in my current job nine months and you may feel it's too early to promote me, but I've learned quickly and I think I have the perfect skills to thrive in this new position," you offer up the negative factor and it becomes diffused. But be sure to give the reason for a yes *last*, says Hogan. People, he reveals, remember what was said last. And the last item has a better shot of winning.

6. Don't bully. Some people put a challenging or threatening spin on their requests, as if they're hoping to scare or intimidate the other person into acquiescing. But that always makes me less receptive, no matter how justified the person may be.

   Recently a young woman sent me a letter asking for a chance to work at the magazine. The letter was fairly compelling—until her closing. She ended with "Someone must have given you the first shot, why not be the one to give me mine." The tone bugged me. Reading the line

"Someone must have given you the first shot" seemed to imply that I'd once been floundering, that I'd perhaps served time in a juvenile facility until a benefactor recognized a kernel of talent in me and helped set me straight. And the last part implied that if I didn't help her, I was being unfair. You must be careful not to put the other person on the defensive.

7. Remember that when someone offers you a job, the salary they initially offer is almost always less than what they're capable of paying. A woman who worked for me has a friend who is a young associate at one of the big accounting firms. A lot of the young associates, both men and women, had started around the same time and had become friends. One night, when they were all out for a drink, they swapped info about their salaries. What a shocker. It turned out that every single woman had accepted the salary she'd been offered, but every guy had asked for more and received it. Say something like, "I'd love to work here, but I was hoping for . . ."

   If they say no, have a backup plan ready. What's *second* best for you? A different job title, perhaps? Ask for that.

8. If you convince yourself not to ask for some reason (they don't have the money, you'll look foolish, etc.), write your excuse down, stash it away for two days, and then take it out. Realize that it is bullshit. Return to #1.

EIGHTY-FIVE

How to Recover from Anything

It probably won't come as any surprise when I tell you that the Confessions column, in which women fess up to their most humiliating, horrifying, and heinous deeds, is one of the highest rated in the magazine. I get such a kick out of reading the copy when it hits my desk every month. Some of the anecdotes involve acts of revenge against evil exes or bosses; others describe hysterically funny hookups. My favorites are always the embarrassing moments, probably because I have never been immune to putting my foot in my mouth or striding through a restaurant oblivious to the fact that I have a pair of panty hose trailing from my pants leg.

It may sometimes seem like there's nothing you can do in a humiliating situation except stand there with a stupefied expression on your face. Consider this story from a reader named Nicole: She and her boyfriend Greg volunteered to spend a weekend caring for her twin nieces so that her sister and brother-in-law could go away for a long weekend. On the first night, after the kids were in bed, Nicole and her boyfriend enjoyed take-out food and a bottle of wine and then started going at it on the couch. Eventually Nicole climbed on top. At one point she looked up and discovered, to her horror, that her nieces had decided to take in the show. The couple quickly dressed, put the girls back to bed, and behaved themselves for the rest of the weekend, figuring all would be forgotten. But when Nicole's sister returned and asked if the twins had had fun, they replied, "Yes, and so did Greg and Nicole. They were bouncing up and down on the couch, and we could see their tushies." What do you *say* at a moment like that?

Well, as speechless as you may be, in most sticky situations it pays to say *something*—because it gives you ownership of the situation and a sense of control. As for what you say, I think there's a basic formula that generally works: go for either funny or forgiveness, depending on the situation.

Funny works in awkward situations in which *you* are the only one experiencing any damage. Humor not only shows that you haven't been undone by the incident, but it also relieves the tension in the room, enabling you to move through the situation so much faster.

Granted, it's hard to conjure up a hilarious remark when you're sweating bullets. So just try to play off the absurdity of the moment. If you realize everyone is gawking at the panty hose trailing from your pants leg, say something like "My mother always told me to travel with a spare pair." If nothing comes to mind, just laugh and say, "Can you believe how hilarious this is?"

When there's been damage to someone else rather than you—for instance, let's say your friend overheard you criticizing her new guy—asking for forgiveness is the only way to go. Apologize swiftly and sincerely and don't try to make light of things. You also don't want to offer lots of excuses, but pleading temporary insanity may make it easier to repair the damage. Example: "I'm so sorry I dissed Rob. I guess I miss seeing you so much that I took it out on him."

EIGHTY-SIX

4 Really Good Stress Busters

Whenever I'm talking to young women about their lives today—whether it's in person or through e-mails or surveys—one common thread I notice is how stressed out they feel.

Initially this came as a surprise to me. I already knew—from personal experience and research while running *Redbook*—that *working moms* are stressed to the max, especially when their kids are small.

A few years ago I noticed that I'd developed scowl lines between my eyes. That took me aback because I didn't think of myself as a scowler. Several months later I was reviewing old vacation photos and discovered one of me scowling in agitation at my then seven-year-old son during a trip to Niagara Falls. We were standing on a path by a modest railing that would supposedly prevent you from falling into the gorge (yeah, right!) and, I instantly remembered, that at the moment of that photo, my son had leaned too close to the railing, looked down into the terrifying gorge, and announced, "It's not so far." *That's* what caused the scowl lines, I suddenly realized. They're from mommy stress.

But why do women without kids and a marriage tend to feel so frazzled?

For one thing, they're under pressure to carve out a certain life for themselves—involving work, love, travel, volunteer activities, exercise—and yet they often feel they don't have enough time to squeeze everything in. And though they now have an abundance of fabulous choices in life, that can be a mixed blessing. Women admit they're nervous about choosing one thing (for instance, the job offer in San Francisco) over another (the cute guy back home) and then regretting their choice.

Stress has become such a big factor among women, in fact, that we've grown accustomed to a certain level of it in our lives. It's sort of like a low-grade flu we walk around with. According to one theory, even when there's nothing currently worthy of our anxiety, we may fret over a minor issue simply because our low-grade stress needs someplace to go. We're what some experts call "stress seekers."

It's no fun to live in a state of heightened stress, but beyond the bad feeling, it can lead to multiple health problems—for instance, headaches, stomach problems, lowered immunity, colds, even perhaps infertility.

And one more thing: as a professional colleague of mine says, when you act really stressed at work, running around in an annoyed or rattled state, looking as if you could come unglued at any moment, you give away your power. To other people, you seem out of control, unfocused, even unreliable.

There's no one cure for stress—you have to attack it from different angles. The starting point is to develop lifestyle habits that make your body better able to endure those slings and arrows of outrageous fortune. If you eat right, exercise regularly, get enough sleep, and don't overdo the double lattes, you're going to feel less hyped up in general and less prone to physical manifestations of anxiety. But no matter how great shape you're in, there will be moments when you feel like flipping out. Here are my four favorite stress busters I've culled from all the research I've looked at over the years:

1. Experiment until you find an instant de-stressor that helps you calm down quickly in a bad situation. Maybe it's something as basic and predictable as counting to ten or taking three deep breaths (research shows that deep breathing really does relax you). Or maybe it's repeating a calming mantra to yourself. One expert we interviewed said that running your fingers lightly along the underside of your arm between the wrist and elbow is amazingly relaxing. An instant de-stressor isn't going to have miraculous results, but it buys you time and lets you think with a clearer head.

2. Resist the urge to "awfulize." I don't think I was aware until I worked at *Cosmo* how profound a tendency women have to imagine the worst. Your boyfriend announces casually over dinner that he's thinking of quitting his job and going to law school, and immediately your mind begins to race—and extrapolate. *He'll never get into a law school around* here, you think, *so he's going to have to go away. What if he ends up on the other side of the country? What if I never see him again? What if this is his way of breaking off the relationship?*

You have to train yourself not to jump too far ahead. Or at least be willing to play out positive scenarios in your head. Maybe he *will* end up in a law school around where you live. And maybe this will light his fire in a terrific way that will be good for both of you. And hey, just think how much money lawyers make! Tell yourself you are only going to react to the news at hand and not skip ahead too far.

3. Go into fact-finding mode. Stress is often heightened because there's an unknown element to the situation—and the unknown can be very scary. You get diagnosed with an STD, for instance, and start to freak because as far as you know, you may as well be an avian flu carrier. You overhear co-workers discussing an upcoming meeting at work that you haven't been invited to and you can't help but worry that you're being boxed out. What you need to do at moments like these is *round up more info.*

This is not jumping ahead and awfulizing. This is knowing all you possibly can about the situation ahead. In some instances we resist fact-finding because we're afraid that the full truth will be even worse than the partial truth we have available at the moment. But from my experience, full knowledge both gives you a wonderful sense of control and relieves your anxiety. Go on the Web and find out everything you can about the STD. Most of them can be treated fairly easily. Pop into your boss's office and ask her in an unchallenging way if you should be attending the meeting. Maybe not including you was simply an oversight. If your exclusion was intentional and you think you should have been there, arrange a time to talk to your boss and find out how she's viewing your performance these days.

One of the most heart-thumping parts of my job is getting the first report on how an issue sold that month on the newsstand. Fortunately my overall record is good, but I do end up with a stinker occasionally. The director of newsstand circulation is always sympathetic in these cases, though occasionally he can't resist breaking the news with a bit of black humor. "You better nail your windows shut," he said once at the beginning of a phone call. Ouch.

Yes, my heart might thump for a minute, but it's been years since I turned panicky over a dud (and trust me, I've never been so wigged out that I felt like leaping from a window). That's because I go into information-gathering mode immediately. I throw the issue down on the floor with the twelve previous ones and look at it with a fresh eye, fresher than when I was creating it. I do research. And in the end I feel I come away with a sense of what women didn't like about the cover. Sure, it's a rotten shame I didn't figure it out while I was composing the cover (wouldn't *that* have been clever?), but I can still use the info going forward. For instance, I know now to never *ever* put a pair of leather pants on the cover again, no matter how buttery they look. That sense of control makes all the difference.

4. Create a secret soother, something you do on a regular basis that brings you a sense of bliss. This isn't something you should save till things get crazy (though you could also do it then). This should be a pleasurable, calming activity you engage in on a regular basis because it keeps your stress set point as low as possible.

Perhaps you can take a walk along the river every week or have an early morning croissant in a coffee shop. Massage seems like a cliché these days but I have to say that having them regularly has been the answer for me. I fell into the habit when I was writing my second mystery, *A Body to Die For*, which was set in a spa. Hey, there was a ton of research required and *somebody* had to do it. I submitted myself to Swedish massages, deep tissue massages, hot stone massages, and massages where oil was poured onto my "third eye." I became addicted, and not just for hedonistic reasons. I found that I felt calmer in general, and even better, I started averaging a cold every three years rather than every six months.

Whatever you decide on, I think there's a plus in keeping it as your little secret. Recently I walked into a charming Greenwich Village restaurant and discovered a writer I know eating by herself. "Are you waiting for someone?" I asked after we'd said our hellos. She explained that she ate lunch once a week in a little café somewhere off the beaten track. And she never told a soul where she was going. She paid cash so that her husband wouldn't find out. She thought he'd find it frivolous. She said she discovered that having the lunch be her secret made it even more enjoyable.

I agree with her. For whatever reason, soothers seem even better when you have them all to yourself.

AFTERWORD

I f you visit the U.S. Senate, you can pick up a brochure entitled "This Month in Senate History," which contains little nuggets of history all pertaining to a certain month. The February brochure features this tidbit:

> February 17, 1906. Following the conviction of two senators on fraud and corruption charges, novelist David Graham Phillips began his nine-part series in *Cosmopolitan* magazine. These articles attracted a wide audience and made the point that large corporations and corrupt state legislators played too large a role in the selection of senators. Phillips's reliance on innuendo and exaggeration soon earned him the scorn of other reformers and President Theodore Roosevelt, who coined the term "muckraker" to describe this kind of overstated and sensationalist journalism. Nonetheless, the series intensified pressures for adoption of a constitutional amendment providing for direct popular election of senators.

A friend sent this brochure to me recently and I went a little bug-eyed when I read it. *Cosmo* was responsible for the popular election of senators? Had we really shaped history this way? It was pretty amazing to discover, though of course, I also had to acknowledge that we hadn't done anything quite so far-reaching and impactful in many years, and the kind of expressions we coin are things like "hottie biscotti" and "iffy stiffy."

And yet the lessons I've learned over the past eight years have been pretty important to me. They've enabled me to make smarter decisions at work, be more thoughtful about my relationships and enjoy my life even more intensely. I hope that at least a few of these lessons will proved helpful to you, too.

Kate White doesn't want to just
help you get ahead.
She also wants you to be the first to
preview her latest mystery.
Smart, sexy sleuth Bailey Weggins is a
heroine you won't soon forget!

Please turn this page
for a peek at her next sizzling mystery.

Lethally Blond

Available in hardcover.

ONE

I t all started with a coincidence. Not one of those totally creepy coincidences that make you feel as if someone has just walked over your grave. In fact, in hindsight I could see that the phone call I received that late summer night wasn't all that unexpected. But at the time it made me catch my breath. And, of course, it was the start of everything awful that happened.

I'd decided to stop by the office that day, something I rarely do on Tuesdays. It was crazy hot for the second week of September, and it would have been nice to just hang on the brick terrace of my apartment in Greenwich Village, chugging a few iced teas. But a new deputy editor had started recently—Valerie, a hyper, edgy chick who left you overwhelmed with an urge to shoot a tranquilizer dart into her ass—and I thought it would be smart to give her some face time. My copy goes through the executive editor, but it's the deputy editor who assigns me most of my stories and often suggests leads for me to follow up on. Since Tuesday is the day after closing, I knew she'd probably have a few minutes to spare. Most of the staff never even gets in before noon that day.

My name is Bailey Weggins, and I'm a reporter for *Buzz*, one of the weekly celebrity gossip magazines that have become like crack cocaine for women under forty these days. Unlike most of the staff, I don't cover the botched marriages and bulimia debates of the stars. Instead, I report on celebrity crime—like when an A-lister hurls a phone at a hotel desk clerk or hires a hit man to shoot his wife.

It's not something I'd ever imagined myself doing. I was a straight crime writer for the ten years after college, but when the job opened up early in the summer, curiousity and a need for a regular gig prodded me to take it.

"Celebrity crime reporter—are you saying it's a specialized area of journalism?" my mother had asked at the time, as if it were not unlike becoming a pediatric neurosurgeon or astrophysicist.

Initially, I was at a disadvantage because I didn't know—excuse the expression—jackshit about celebrities. Oh, I'd picked up tidbits about the really major stars—you know, like Brad and Angelina and Gwyneth and TomKat—from listening to friends dish as well as perusing gossip magazines during pedicures. But I was clueless about most of the others. In fact, until two weeks into my job at *Buzz*, I'd thought Jake Gyllenhaal and Orlando Bloom were the *same person*. But I caught on pretty quickly, and to my surprise, I grew to really enjoy my two-to-three-day-a-week arrangement. Celebrities not only live large, they misbehave large, too. Covering their crimes, I discovered, could be awfully entertaining.

The place was practically tomblike when I stepped off the elevator, though it was mercifully cool, as if the low body count had prevented the air from rising above sixty-two degrees that day. I nodded to a few people as I walked through the huge cube farm/newsroom that constitutes a big chunk of our offices. I'm in a part of the newsroom nicknamed the Pod, which abuts the art and production departments and houses many of the writers and junior editors. The senior editors are in glass-fronted offices that rim the area. My workstation is right next to a writer named Jessie Pendergrass and behind Leo, a photo editor they couldn't find room for in the photo department.

"Hey," I said to Leo as I tossed my purse and tote bag onto my desk. He was the only one in the general vicinity. He tore his eyes off his computer screen and swiveled just his head toward me.

"To what do we owe this honor?" he asked. "I thought you weren't coming in today."

"I had a few things I wanted to take care of. Jessie around?"

"She's not in yet. I heard her tell someone on the phone yesterday that her bikini line was a disaster, so maybe she's having it administered to."

"Anything going on here?"

"Not really. Oh, there was a little bit of a dustup this morning. You know how we said Britney Spears looked like a Smurf?"

"No. Okay, I'll take your word for it."

"Nash got a phone call today," he said referring to Nash Nolan, the editor in chief. "And the fur was flying."

"From Britney's publicist?"

"No, it was from a *Smurf* representative. They don't want to be compared to her."

"Very funny. So what are you working on?" I sidled over to his desk and checked out the computer screen. There was a grainy shot of a blond starlet type I didn't recognize sitting at an outdoor restaurant jamming half a dozen French fries into her mouth as if she were stuffing clothes into an overfilled hamper. "God, the paparazzi don't let these chicks alone, do they," I said.

"The ones who take these shots don't consider themselves paparazzi," he said. "They're *snackarazzi*."

"You're kidding, right?"

"Not at all. These are the real money shots these days. They are even better than a star scratching her ass."

"Remind me not to order a double bacon cheeseburger the next time I'm at a sidewalk café."

"I think *you're* safe, Bailey."

I checked my e-mail and then a bunch of Web sites to see if any A-listers had landed themselves in hot water that day, but things seemed fairly quiet. After grabbing a cup of coffee, I wandered down to the office of the new deputy editor.

"Hi, Val," I said, poking my head in the door and forcing a smile. I've always wished I were good at office politics, but fawning and bullshitting just don't come easily to me, particularly if the person at the other end is a real jerk, which I suspected Valerie was. A guy I used to work with at the *Albany Times Union*, back in my postcollege days, said that I buttkissed about as well as a blowtorch.

"What can I do for you?" Valerie asked without enthusiasm. Her dark brown hair was brushed off her face, unfortunately accenting the sharpness of her nose and the pea size of her eyes. She reminded me of how our family dog used to look when he emerged sopping wet from a pond.

"Just thought I'd check in—see if you needed me for anything," I told her.

"What are you working on now?" she asked, a thin layer of impatience coating her question.

Gosh, I thought, you just don't like me, *do* you? But I couldn't tell why. She'd arrived at the magazine during a tumultuous period, not long after the editor in chief had been killed. She'd inherited the place of the previous deputy editor who'd taken over for Nash when he was crowned editor in chief. I wondered if she resented the fact that Nash and I were tight.

"Nothing major at the moment," I told her. "Just following a few leads. I probably won't come in again this week unless something breaks."

"Just let Aubrey know," she said, referring to the managing editor. Then she glanced over at her computer screen as if she was dying to get back to work.

"Sure," I said and walked off. How nice that I'd bothered to take the subway up from the Village.

As long as I was at the office, I followed up with staffers on a few matters and polished off another cup of coffee. And then, with nothing more to do, I stood up to go.

"Oh, Bailey, I know what your favorite TV show is going to be this season," Leo said as I was shutting off my computer. "Have you seen the fall lineup?"

"No, but let me guess. *Fear Factor: Marriage*?"

"Nope. A new show called *Morgue*. It's about forensic investigators from the medical examiner's office. Sounds perfect for someone with your grisly interests."

"Aren't there a million shows like that already?" I asked.

"I guess the public just can't get enough of them."

Just to humor him, I sauntered over to Leo's desk and glanced down at his computer screen. Along with the description of the show, there were a few shots from episodes and a group photo of the ensemble cast, all perfectly coiffed and smileless, their eyes burning with desire to see justice done and have the show score a fifteen share. Suddenly I felt my jaw drop. One of the actors I was staring at in the ensemble cast was Chris Wickersham. He was a model and actor I'd had a short fling with in the late winter.

"Oh my," I said.

"What—you think you're really gonna like it?"

"No, the guy on the far left. I know him."

"Really?" He said as he glanced back at the screen. "You mean—Chris Wickersham, who plays Jared Hanson, the sometimes moody but brilliantly intuitive investigator? Is he straight?"

"Very. It says it's about the New York City Morgue. Does that mean it's shooting here?"

"Not necessarily. Lemme see . . . yes, shot entirely in New York City. Was this guy your boyfriend?"

"Sort of. For about four seconds. Is there anything else?"

"No, just that it premieres September twenty-first."

"Look, I'd better fly. Tell Jessie hi for me, will you?"

I grabbed my purse and tote bag and headed out of the building. My mind was racing, thinking of what I'd just learned about Chris. The last time I had laid eyes on him was right before he'd struck out for L.A. last March hoping, like millions of other guys with perfect jawlines, to be cast in a pilot for the fall. We hadn't said anything about staying in touch (though early on he'd sent two e-mails and one goofy postcard of the Hollywood sign), and I'd just assumed he hadn't met with any real success yet. But he had. And based on the public love of carnage and corpses, there was every chance the show would be a success. I felt happy for Chris. He deserved fame and glory. But at the same time there was something vaguely disconcerting about the whole thing that I couldn't put my finger on. Maybe it was knowing that a guy I'd locked lips with was now poised to become the kind of hottie who women across America drooled over and discussed the next day at the water cooler.

I took the subway to Eighth and Broadway, hit the gym for thirty minutes, scarfed up a few supplies at the deli, and then headed to my apartment. Though I'd only left home a few hours earlier, my apartment was stifling hot. I turned on the AC, fixed an ice water, and flopped on the couch. As I took the first sip of my drink, I let memories of Chris Wickersham run roughshod around my brain. I had met him two Aprils ago at a wedding, where he had worked as one of the bartenders, supplementing the money he made from modeling and small acting gigs. He was absolutely gorgeous, the kind of guy who it almost hurt to look at.

Though he took my number and called me, I'd blown him off. He was ten years younger than me and despite the fact that that kind of age gap hadn't bothered Cameron Diaz and Demi Moore, I just couldn't imagine having a boyfriend who I was old enough to have babysat for. Then, nine months later, we'd reconnected when I'd needed his help during a murder investigation. I was dating someone steadily by then, and I tried not to send any of the wrong messages to Chris, but one night he had kissed me and I'd felt it all the way to my tippy toes. It was the beginning of my doubts about my existing relationship. Soon afterwards I was single again. Chris and I embarked on six or seven dates and some serious makeout sessions, but I'd been unable to take the relationship—sexual and otherwise—beyond that. One of the last things Chris had said to me was, "Christ, Bailey, what *is* it with you—yes or no?" In the end it had been no. In hindsight I thought my doubts might have been due to guilt. I always associated Chris with my breakup.

If I met him today, would I still feel those doubts? I wondered. What would it be like to date a guy who millions of people watched on TV? Christ, Bailey, I thought. You're starting to sound like a starfucker.

I drained the last of my water. I'd planned to stay in tonight to work on a freelance article. Plus, ever since I had my heart bruised during the summer by a guy name Beau Regan, I'd been laying low. But thanks to the heat wave, the idea now held nada appeal. I wondered whom I might be able to drum up for companionship on short notice. My seventy-year-old next-door neighbor Landon, who I sometimes palled around with, had said he was heading over to the Film Forum on West Houston to see a German flick. A college pal of mine from Brown had recently split with her husband and she was game for anything that provided escape from her apartment, but an evening in her company could be exhausting. She tended to ask an endless series of borderline-hostile questions that were impossible for me to answer—like "Are all men dickheads or just the ones I meet?", "Who would drink a prickly pear martini, do you know?", and "Do *you* think I'm brimming with anger?".

Maybe I would just head out alone and eat a quiet dinner outdoors at one of the restaurants over on McDougal. As I padded toward my bedroom to change, my cell phone buzzed from my purse, making me jump.

"Hello," I said after digging it out.

"Bailey?"

"Yes."

"Hi, it's Chris Wickersham."

For a brief moment I thought it was Leo playing a practical

joke. But he wouldn't have been familiar with that deep, smooth voice—and so I knew for certain it had to be Chris.

"Oh my gosh," I said. "I—I was just reading about you two hours ago. Congratulations—I, er, heard about the show." God, Bailey, this is why you *write* professionally, I thought. You shouldn't be allowed to open your mouth.

"Thanks," he said. "The opportunity kind of came out of nowhere. I've been planning to call you—I mean, just to say hello."

"So you're back in New York?"

"Yeah—I've got a studio in Tribeca. I don't want to overextend myself until I know if the show is going to take off or not."

"Is the shooting schedule as brutal as you hear?"

"Fourteen-hour days. But this is what I wanted and I've got no complaints. The show kicks in two weeks and then we play the ratings game."

"It sounds like a super idea for a show—I'm sure it will be a hit."

"Kind of your type of show, huh?"

"You're the second person who said that today."

"Well look, the reason I called . . . I mean, I wanted to say hi, but—is there any chance you could meet me for a drink? There's a matter I need to talk to you about."

"Sure," I said. His tone didn't suggest a man who'd been pining for me for months and had decided to make one last stab at winning my heart, but I was still curious. "When were you thinking?"

"I know this is short notice, but I was wondering if you could do it now. It's really pretty urgent. You're the one person who I can turn to on this."

"What is it? Are you in some kind of trouble?"

"No, no. But a friend of mine may be. I need your advice."

"Can you give me a hint?" I asked, though I figured that if a guy he knew was in trouble, it had to involve drugs or money or both.

"It—look, would you mind talking about it in person? I hate the idea of starting to get into it on the phone and then having to cover the same ground again when we meet."

"Well, I could do it *now* actually," I admitted. "I was planning to stay in and work tonight, but it can wait."

"That's terrific," he said. He suggested we meet in an hour and asked me to recommend a place near me. I threw out the name of a bar on Tenth Street near Second Avenue.

After signing off, I walked distractedly into the bathroom and splashed cool water on my face and my armpits. I couldn't believe what had just happened. Maybe it was my destiny that Chris Wickersham would pop into my life every nine months or so. I wondered if there was any chance that he was using a so-called problem with a friend as an excuse to make contact with me. It had been hard to tell on the phone. And I wasn't at all sure how I'd feel when I saw him. I had never once stopped finding him staggeringly attractive. Perhaps now that I was no longer guilt-stricken—and my love life was currently in the Dumpster with a capital D—I would feel the urge to go for it this time.

Covering my bets, I wore a pair of tight jeans and a flowy turquoise baby doll top with a fairly deep V. I smoothed my blondish brown hair and applied just enough eye shadow, mascara, blush, and lip gloss to keep from looking as if I'd tried as hard as I had.

He wasn't in the bar when I arrived. I found a free table by the front window and ordered a Corona. Taking a sip of the icy cold beer from the bottle, I watched people stroll along the pavement in the September dusk. A couple of guys stared through the glass at me and one even shot me a big smile. I realized suddenly how nice it was to be sitting in a kind of slutty top, waiting for a hunk— even if it wasn't really a date. Along with my heart, my ego had been bruised by Beau Regan. This was the closest I'd felt in ages to being a bitch on wheels.

"Hey, Bailey, hi."

It was Chris's voice behind me. He must have entered the bar without my seeing him.

As I shifted in my chair, I caught two women gazing at a spot behind me, their mouths agape. As soon as I spun around I could see why. Chris Wickersham had somehow managed to become even more gorgeous in the months since I'd last seen him. He'd gained a few pounds, filling out his face in the nicest of ways. His sandy brown hair was little longer and tinged with blond highlights. The biceps were the same, though. They cockily stretched the sleeves of a gray T-shirt he wore over tan cargo shorts. Had I been the stupidest girl in America to reject him?

I stood up to greet Chris and at the same moment he leaned forward to kiss me on the cheek. Because of the awkward angle of our bodies, the edge of his full mouth touched mine, and I felt the same rush I'd experienced the very first time he'd kissed me in Miami. Take it down, way down, Bailey, I told myself. I had no idea what Chris's intentions were—or mine for that matter—and I didn't want to get ahead of myself.

"Hey there," was all I could muster.

"God, it's great to see those blue eyes again, Bailey. You look amazing."

"Well, I'm not the one with half the bar staring at me."

"I'll start describing what we do in the morgue with a Stryker saw and let's see how they like that," he said grinning. He made a dead-on whiny saw noise that made me laugh out loud.

He ordered a beer for himself and we talked for a few minutes about the series. It was being shot entirely in New York, with all the interior morgue shots done at a soundstage at Chelsea Piers. He interrupted himself at one point to ask how my work was going, and I told him about being dumped by *Gloss* and miraculously finding the gig at *Buzz*.

"Gosh, is it dangerous for me to be talking to you now that you work for a celebrity rag?" he asked, his eyes playful.

"Only if you hurl your phone at someone or start groping girls on the streets of Manhattan." I took a swig of beer, thinking of a zillion other questions I had about the series, but before I could ask a single one, Chris switched gears on us.

"Like I said on the phone," he said, lowering his voice slightly, "I wanted to talk to you about this friend of mine. I really appreciate your meeting me."

Omigod, I suddenly thought, the "friend" is a girl. He's got chick trouble and he wants my advice, like I'm some sort of big sister. I felt a flush of embarrassment begin to creep up my chest.

"Okay, tell me about it," I said awkwardly.

"It's about this actor I know—named Tom Fain. We met doing an off-off-Broadway show a year or two ago, and he ended up in *Morgue* too. He's just got a small part but he's generally in every episode."

"Is he in some kind of trouble?" I asked, feeling oddly relieved that it was a guy friend after all. I waited for a tale of woe that would probably include at least one long weekend in Vegas.

"I guess you'd call it that," Chris said. "He's missing."

"*Missing?*" I exclaimed.

"Yeah, he disappeared off the face of the earth a week and a half ago."

"Have you talked to the police—of course, they're not much help with young guys."

"The first person I called was this guy who Tom had mentioned—Mr. Barish—who handled the money. He said he'd get a hold of the cops. This detective called me a day later. He looked around the apartment and said he'd make a couple of inquiries but there was nothing more he could really do," he said. He said a lot of guys just take off. But I don't think that's what happened. This was his first regular TV gig. He's a couple of years older than me and he's been praying for this break even longer than I have. I just don't believe he would have walked away from it."

"Is there a girlfriend in the picture? Could he have had a blowup and gone off to lick his wounds?"

"There's a kind of girlfriend, a chick named Harper he's been seeing for about a month and a half. She's a former actress who does PR for the show. But it's not some major love affair, and she's just as clueless as I am about where he is."

"Parents?"

"Both dead. You ready for another?" he asked, cocking his chin toward my beer.

I'd noticed that he'd chugged his own down quickly, feeling churned up perhaps from talking about Tom. I was only halfway through mine.

"I'm set for now. So tell me the circumstances. When did you last see Tom? When did *anyone* last see him?"

"I talked to him the Thursday before he disappeared. We were on set together. He plays—or I should say *played* because it looks like they've canned him—this guy who mans the phones at the morgue, the one who's always handing someone a message or announcing that so-and-so is on line four. I'm not sure what he did the next day because they didn't need him on set, but apparently on Saturday morning he picked up his car from a lot downtown and took off. Harper was out of town that weekend but she talked to Tom Friday night and he didn't mention anything about a trip. *Originally* he'd been planning to head out to Long Island to see this buddy of his, but the guy told me the plans got bagged late in the week. When Tom didn't show for work on Monday, I kept trying to reach his cell phone, and finally went to his apartment. As far as I know, no one's heard from him since that weekend."

"Was he depressed—or in any kind of trouble that you know of?"

"Not that I know of. He's a helluva nice guy. He actually suggested I audition for the show."

He drew his fist to his face and blew a stream of air into it. I waited, thinking he was going to say something else, but he only stared at me expectantly.

"How can I help?" I asked. I had no idea what I could possibly do, but I assumed that was the question Chris had been waiting for.

"I want you to tell me how I can I find him. You solve mysteries, right? I just want some direction."

I sighed. "When I'm writing a story—or when I'm working on a case like the one I needed your help on last winter—I find that the best approach is to just methodically turn over every stone, one by one. It's not very sexy-sounding and yet it's usually the best way. But I don't know anything about Tom's life, so I wouldn't know which stones to start with."

"I can help with that. I can tell you everything I know about him. Plus, I have a key to his apartment. He was nice enough to let me bunk there for a few weeks this summer and I thought if you looked through it with me, we might find something—a lead."

"Uh, sure," I said. That was certainly more than providing a "little direction" but I was intrigued, and I liked being with Chris. "That would certainly be a start. When?"

"How about right now?"

"*Now*? Well, why not, I guess? Even though you've got a key to the place, is there anyone who could make trouble for you if they caught you there?"

"No. Like I said, the parents are dead, he's got no siblings, and the super is used to me being around."

"Okay, then. Let's do it."

He waved for the check, paid, and three minutes later we were out on the street. He said Tom lived on Mercer so we headed there on foot. While we walked, Chris provided more details about Tom. He'd grown up in Manhattan, gone to private school, and then majored in theater at Skidmore College. Whereas Chris had used modeling as a potential springboard for acting and had eventually headed to L.A., Tom had plugged away mostly in the off-off-Broadway world, performing in many small "black box" theaters, once totally nude.

I was curious, I told Chris, about the guy Tom had said he was going to see on Long Island. Was there a chance Tom *had* headed out there and the guy was denying it? Perhaps he and Tom had ended up in an altercation, or at the very least this dude was covering up something. Chris didn't think so. The guy was an old high school friend of Tom's.

The building was modern and well kept, no doorman, but a nice lobby. Not exactly what I was expecting for an actor who until recently had done five-dollar-a-ticket theaters and let his schlong dangle in front of an audience. Reading my mind, Chris explained that Tom had purchased his place with money from the sale of his parents' apartment on the Upper East Side.

We took the elevator to four and I followed Chris down a long hallway, the walls painted a tobacco color and hung with brass sconces. From the pocket of his shorts he pulled a set of keys and thumbed through several until he found the one to Chris's place. He turned the lower Medico lock and then, when that was unlocked, a top one. I was right behind him as he pushed the door open and no sooner had he stopped into the vestibule when I felt his body tense.

I soon knew why: In a room at the very end of the hall, probably the bedroom, a light was glowing. Someone seemed to be home.